Praise for He

"In the pages of *Hello Mornings*, Kat Lee speaks to you right where you are in life and encourages you to be all that God created you to be in words that are covered in grace and humor because Kat knows how much we all have on our plates as we walk through life. Kat will make you laugh out loud, breathe a deep sigh of relief, and re-evaluate the way you start your day."

—Melanie Shankle, *New York Times* bestselling author

"I want to give this book to all the women I know. It is a rare treasure. The principles described will transform your life by motivating you to understand how to have a deep, meaningful relationship with God by studying His Word; and to live life knowing His love, wisdom, and purpose every day and through all your seasons."

—Sally Clarkson, author, *The Lifegiving Home* and *Different*

"Do you desire consistency and rhythm in your life but are struggling to make that desire a reality? Kat Lee has written a manual that will help you develop the mind-set and intentional habits necessary to meet your day proactively instead of reacting to your day when you wake up.

"*Hello Mornings* is more than a book of how-tos. It is tried-and-true experience backed with research that will help you stay connected to God, stay ahead of your day, and stay in charge of your body. This is a book of practical encouragement no woman should be without!"

—Chrystal Evans Hurst, author, *She's Still There* and *Kingdom Woman*

"With compassion, grace and inspiration, Kat Lee leads us to what our hearts long for most: freedom. With each page, readers can cast off discouragement and burdens and discover the joy of living intentionally for ourselves, our families, and God. *Hello Mornings* is a gift and a joy straight from Kat's heart."

—Tricia Goyer, bestselling
author, *Walk It Out*

"The power of *Hello Mornings* is not just ideas, devotionals, and concepts. It is from someone who has literally lived out everything she is challenging us all to do. Whether you are single, newlywed, a young mom, or further along in the journey, this book and devotional journey is for you."

—Jimmy Seibert, senior pastor,
Antioch Community Church

"Waking up *for* my life and not *to* my life is a game-changing concept. Kat walks us through how to make this a reality in our day-to-day lives, and I'm certain that your days will be smoother after reading this book."

—Jamie Ivey, podcast host, *The
Happy Hour with Jamie Ivey*,
and author, *If You Only Knew*

"I have long admired Kat Lee for her unwavering commitment to morning time and the impact it has on our entire day. Now she takes her most learned lessons and teaches us how to practically live them out in our own lives. If saying hello to the morning is a struggle for you as it has been for me, this book is for you!"

—Ruth Schwenk, founder,
TheBetterMom.com; and
coauthor, *Pressing Pause*

"No matter what season you're in, *Hello Mornings* will help you start your days on purpose. I love Kat's down-to-earth advice and friendly encouragement. This book makes me want to wake up."

—Sarah Mackenzie, author,
The Read-Aloud Family, and
founder, Read-Aloud Revival

"I plan to have stacks of *Hello Mornings* handy to give anyone overwhelmed by daily demands. These pages hold encouraging stories, gentle grace, and solid statistics, not only to inspire but equip. As your personal coach, Kat helps you form habits to transform your life from the inside out."

—Heather MacFadyen, podcast
host, *The God-Centered Mom*

"As a lifelong night owl, I've always known that I could better maximize my mornings—and I've often berated myself for failing to do so. Instead of heaping guilt on her readers, Kat Lee comes along like a gentle guide who lays out a plan for waking up early enough to spend time with God, plan for each day, and incorporate gentle exercise. Her emphasis on persistence over perfection will set up even the latest of night owls for success."

—Erin Odom, author, *More Than
Just Making It* and *You Can
Stay Home with Your Kids*

"I am thrilled you have this book in your hands. Do not put it down. Start this journey immediately, and let Kat help you revolutionize your days through the proven principles in *Hello Mornings*. For years she has coached thousands of women, using right motivations, timely encouragement, and important biblical truths. God has gifted Kat with the ability to lovingly and effectively light a fire in the lives of women who want to experience productive, joy-filled days."

—Katie Orr, author, FOCUSed15
Bible studies

"Reading *Hello Mornings*, you'll be inspired, encouraged, and challenged. With simple, yet profound directives, Kat Lee will usher your heart and life toward greater depth, wellness, and faith. Her stories, suggestions, and biblical conversations will have you laughing, crying, believing, and behaving in freshly beautiful ways. Each page is an adventurous path to Jesus, who masterfully loves and redeems."

—Gwen Smith, author, *I Want It ALL*
and *Broken into Beautiful*; and
cofounder, Girlfriends in God

hello mornings

hello mornings

HOW TO BUILD
A GRACE-FILLED, LIFE-GIVING
MORNING ROUTINE

kat lee

W PUBLISHING GROUP

AN IMPRINT OF THOMAS NELSON

Published in Nashville, Tennessee, by W Publishing Group, an imprint of Thomas Nelson.

Published in association with the literary agency D. C. Jacobson & Associates, LLC, an author management company.

Thomas Nelson titles may be purchased in bulk for educational, business, fund-raising, or sales promotional use. For information, please e-mail SpecialMarkets@ThomasNelson.com.

ISBN 978-0-7180-9366-2 (eBook)

Library of Congress Cataloging-in-Publication Data

Names: Lee, Kat, author.
Title: Hello mornings : how to build a grace-filled, life-giving morning
   routine / Kat Lee.
Description: Nashville : W Publishing Group, 2017. | Includes bibliographical
   references.
Identifiers: LCCN 2017026672 | ISBN 9780718094171 (trade paper)
Subjects: LCSH: Christian women—Religious life. | Spiritual life—
   Christianity. | Prayer—Christianity. | Bible—Reading. | Spiritual exercises.
Classification: LCC BV4527 .L447 2017 | DDC 248.8/43—dc23 LC record available
   at https://lccn.loc.gov/2017026672

Printed in the United States of America

17 18 19 20 21 LSC 6 5 4 3 2

To Jimmy, Anna, Allison, and Jackson.
I just spent an entire year and more than two hundred
pages writing about a simple three-minute morning routine.
How can I possibly consolidate my love and gratitude
for my sweet family into one tiny paragraph? So, for
now, just know that I love you with my whole heart.

(And when I finally craft the perfect
dedication, I'll tape it on the fridge.)

Let the morning bring me word of your unfailing love,
    for I have put my trust in you.
Show me the way I should go,
    for to you I entrust my life.

—Psalm 143:8

Contents

part one

Why Mornings?

one

Setting the Stage

In the 1992 Barcelona Olympics, Derek Redmond was Great Britain's best hope for a medal in the four-hundred-meter race. At the semifinals, everyone expected him to qualify for the finals. He lined up for his event. The gun went off; Derek charged around the track, fending off the other runners.

But at the two-hundred-meter mark, Derek collapsed in a heap on the ground, writhing in pain. As the other contestants passed him by, leaving his dreams in their dust, Derek wrestled with the realization and pain of a ripped hamstring.

Everything he had worked for his entire life had just ended. In an instant, his failure was complete.

Derek wouldn't win the race. He wouldn't win an Olympic medal. He would need to be carried off on a stretcher. He didn't meet his own expectations or anyone else's. He could have labeled himself a failure in that moment, but he wrote a better story. He refused to quit.

As the other runners approached the finish, Derek struggled to his feet, gripped his leg, and with tears running down his face, began hobbling toward the finish line more than two hundred meters away. He couldn't win, but he could finish. He took excruciating step after excruciating step, determined to complete his race.

Slowly the crowd realized what was happening. A wave of cheers spread throughout the stadium, and, by the hundreds, spectators rose to their feet. The announcers barely acknowledged the winner of the race, too choked up with emotion and focused on the greater story happening at two hundred meters.

Then, something even more incredible happened. There was a small commotion in the crowd. A man who was a little older and a little grayer than Derek pushed his way down to the railing. He jumped over the railing onto the track and fought off security guards and officials as he ran to his broken and beaten son. Derek's father wrapped his arms around him in support and spoke words of love, hope, and courage over him. You could see the relief wash over Derek as his father helped him carry his pain.

Together, they crossed the finish line.

Later, reporters swarmed the elder Mr. Redmond and asked what inspired him to push through the crowd, fight past security, and jump onto the track with his son. Mr. Redmond simply said, "I intended to go over the line with him. We started his career together; I think we should finish it together."[1]

Friends, I don't know where you are in your journey with God. I don't know how many times you've tried to spend time with Him or read the Word or prayed and felt as if you failed. But I do know that He does not merely stand at the finish line awaiting your triumphant victory. Our loving God, our faithful Father, is fighting to come alongside you in the journey. To push past all the discouragements and distractions. To speak words of love, hope, and courage over you. To wrap His arms around you and finish the race with you. Because of Jesus, God does not require our perfection; He wants a relationship with us. That's what this book is all about. If I help you build the habit of connecting with Him every day, no matter how broken and beaten you may feel, I know He can take you the rest of the way. He can heal, He can restore, He can redeem, and He wants you to be a part of a great and powerful story.

The God of heaven and earth wants to come alongside you each and every day and run your race with you, starting first thing in the morning. Maybe you've tried waking up early before. Maybe you're in a season that makes mornings challenging. But please know this: creating a life-giving morning routine is so much simpler than we are often led to believe.

As the founder of HelloMornings.org, I've seen thousands of women in countries around the world build lasting morning routines that start their days well—routines that impact their hearts, their communities, and the world around them. They weren't born "morning people," and you don't have to be one either. You don't need to wake up at the crack of dawn. You don't need to lose sleep or even set your alarm. *What? How is that possible?* That's what we're going to learn together.

You'll meet women just like you—women in every stage, season, and situation of life—who have found a way to make mornings work for them. I'll share my story and help you understand yours, and together we'll build a new morning routine for you. I'll show you how you can begin a long-term investment in your life that will influence not only you but also those around you. You'll understand the process of building a lasting morning routine, read stories, and learn the science behind how God-centered, small, simple habits can transform your life. And we'll begin with a step-by-step, three-minute morning routine. Everyone has three minutes.

What to Expect from This Book

I'd like to give you a little roadmap of what's ahead in this book. I've divided *Hello Mornings* into three parts. The first part introduces you to why mornings are important, the second gives you a blueprint for your daily routine, and the third part offers tools to help make your morning routine a consistent part of your life.

If you want a crazy hard, complex solution, this isn't the book for you. If you want a quick fix, this isn't the book for you. If you want a simple, scalable solution that leads to a deeper relationship with God and permanent personal change, then keep reading.

Keep in mind as you read that the inspiration doesn't end with this book. Our thriving online community at HelloMornings .org will keep your morning routine going strong. We're here to answer your questions, keep you motivated, and learn new things together.

The Solution (yep, right here in chapter 1)

You picked up this book because you need a solution for your mornings—your life—so I'm going to give it to you here in chapter 1. The best part? It only takes three minutes. As you read, you'll begin to understand the power of such a simple routine. You'll learn in later chapters how to scale it up. And you'll learn how to keep it going.

The Three-Minute Morning
1. Read / memorize / pray Psalm 143:8.
2. Look at your calendar for today.
3. Drink a glass of water.

There you go. That will change your life. There's nothing magical about each step, yet each one is crucial. Feel boxed in by how specific it is? You can change it up, but I recommend you understand the purpose behind each item first by reading through the rest of this book. Do you already have a morning routine? Great! Add this. You'll learn why and how adding something small can make a big difference.

Three minutes can change everything. Start now.

Remember: everyone has three minutes. It's what you do with them that can make all the difference. For me? It took me around the world and back.

My Story

My name is Kat Lee. It's nice to meet you! If we were sitting down for coffee, you'd quickly learn that I'm a forty-something, half-Asian Texan who loves sports, office supplies, and coffee. If you're into Myers-Briggs, I'm an ENFP (an extroverted, intuitive, feeling perceiver). I love planning and organization, but

I'm not naturally neat and tidy. I'm passionate about people, and I absolutely love cheering on others. If I were standing next to you right now, I'd be whisper-cheering, "You can do this! I'm so proud of you! Keep reading! Go, you!" I might even be holding a big sign or banner with your name on it. Think "adorkable" rather than "stalkerish."

I started being intentional about my mornings after marriage and family filled my days. This isn't a mom book, but I have to tell you: the way my life has unfolded is a core part of the story God has written for me. He has woven redemption and restoration into my years in unexpected ways. And all along this bumpy road, I've felt His hand on the small of my back, gently leading me at each turn. I'll share some of those twists and turns because my motherhood story and my morning story are inextricably woven together. I pray you'll find hope for your story and vision for your mornings.

Her name was Cristina, and she was beautiful. She had an olive complexion, brown Filipina eyes, and a petite frame. She could sing like an angel. She was my mother. She loved Jesus and my daddy, and I've been told she loved me too. I'd like to think so. But I never heard her say it—at least not that I remember, because just nine months after I came into the world, her illness-ridden body left it.

Motherhood was always a mystery to me. What was it like to call someone Mom? To see her eyes light up? To call her name and have her comfort me when I was sad or sick? To say it with entitled ingratitude knowing my emotions were safe with her? What was it like to be able to look into the eyes of the woman I'd someday become? *Mother*. Such a simple, universal word . . . that I'd never fully understand.

It was the small things I missed the most. I didn't hold her hand on my first day of school as I crossed the street in front of Komarek Elementary. I didn't wiggle around as she tried to brush the knots out of my hair. I didn't argue with her about my clothes I didn't roll my eyes, ignoring motherly advice to put a jacket on before going out to play in the crisp Chicago air. I didn't ask her if she knew the secret to good, tight-rolled jeans.

My mama was a nurse, they told me. She was from the Philippines and met my blond-haired, blue-eyed father at a get-together in Chicago that my aunt hosted. Growing up, I don't think I could have told you the difference between the words *Philippians* and *Philippines*. I'm sure I confused the two more than once. My mom had been the only member of her family to come to the United States, so I knew absolutely nothing about Filipino culture and very little about my other family on the opposite side of the world. I grew up with my Swedish-Dutch dad and his side of the family.

But I'd heard a few names: Lolo and Lola, my grandparents. Aunt Rufe. Cousin Esther Sandee. I even got a few airmailed letters. But that was about it. I wasn't sure how they were all related exactly. How many brothers and sisters did my mom have? What were their names? How many cousins did I have? I had no idea. So much about my mother was a mystery to me.

Few things highlighted my ignorance more than the second Sunday of May. No one thought much about the little girl who always threw her Mother's Day craft in the trash on the way out of Sunday school. Holding back tears, I looked around at all the moms and daughters and felt as though I was on the outside looking in on a relationship that I would never know.

But I was never alone. Just like Derek Redmond's father, God walked alongside me in my pain. He brought women into my life to show me how to live. And as I followed Him along the journey, He orchestrated a beautiful and redemptive plot twist that I would never have known if I hadn't been walking with Him day by day.

She was born in June 2002. My husband, Jimmy, and I were parents of a precious little girl. I was a mother. I was a *mother*. We named her Anna, and she was beautiful, just like my mama.

God redeems.

But He wasn't done.

Allison, my mini-me, was born two years later. I felt a little like Job at the end of his story when he received back twofold all he had lost. I had not only one but two precious daughters. Two opportunities to experience that elusive relationship I thought I'd never know. Two opportunities to be the very thing I always dreamed of having. And two beautiful reasons to look forward to Mother's Day.

God redeems.

But He still wasn't done.

We have three children now. Jackson was born in 2007, and he is a joy. I know I make mistakes, but I'm also fighting every single day to be all God dreamed when He chose me to be the mother of my three children. I'll be the first to admit I have no earthly idea what I'm doing. I just know I desperately need Jesus moment by moment. Apart from Him, I'll hurt these beautiful children He has entrusted to me. Apart from Him, I'll be apathetic. Apart from Him, I'll set my expectations too high and pass on the pain of my childhood.

But I don't really mind being inadequate because it's a daily reminder of my need for Jesus. I can't be wise enough, patient enough, or loving enough, but in Christ, I can do all things (Phil. 4:13).

Early on in motherhood, I learned to fall at His feet first. I learned to let Him fill me before I tried to fill anyone else. That's how my morning routine started: just a prayer and a few verses.

And that one simple, small habit has taken me places I never would have imagined. To a deeper relationship with God than I'd dreamed. To a messy and wild life that feels peacefully well anchored. And into a story of redemption that brings encouragement and hope to others.

I started a mom blog in 2010, when my children were seven, five, and two, and I found it deeply ironic. Who was I to start a mom blog? Not only was I clueless about motherhood, I was also not your typical mom. I hate cooking. When anyone mentions the word *crafts*, I end up in the fetal position in a corner rocking back and forth. Give me a ball and something to throw, kick, or shoot it into, and I'm happy as a clam.

But I was passionate about the nobility of motherhood. I knew the power of a mother's influence—positive or negative, present or absent. A mother's impact is undeniable. I clearly felt God calling me to speak encouragement to moms.

The motherless mom blogger. It didn't make sense, but God doesn't usually pick the obvious choices.

When I started my blog, the first thing I wrote about was my morning routine. I made it into an e-book, actually. I shared how I'd wake up before the kids and what I did in my morning time. Riveting, right? I am a party wherever I go. A wild one, I am.

But, very unexpectedly, that e-book was shared far and wide. Eventually, a reader asked if we could do a group challenge based on that morning routine. We called it Hello Mornings, and, over the years, thousands and thousands of women have joined together and encouraged one another in the journey.

By fall 2010, the blog was doing really well. So well, in fact, that I got a message from Shaun Groves, the director of the Compassion Bloggers program.

Compassion is a child sponsorship program that our family has been involved with for years. At the time, their blogger program selected writers to take on trips around the world to show what Compassion does to help children. I'd followed every single one of their trips because some of my favorite writers went and shared their experiences. I wept buckets at Ann Voskamp's stories and laughed at the adventures of Melanie Shankle, and I added a new sponsor child almost every trip I followed. Now it was my turn—Shaun invited me to go with them on their next trip.

———————

Growing up, we weren't a world-traveling family. Sometimes we'd drive up to Green Lake, Wisconsin, during the summers or visit Uncle Merl and Aunt June on their farm in Indiana, but we never flew anywhere. I had friends who went overseas, but I never imagined myself in far-flung places.

But there I was. The motherless mom blogger with an opportunity to use my words to help children. I was honored.

I reread Shaun's message several times to make sure it was meant for me.

But his next message left me undone. My husband, Jimmy, was out of town, the kids were asleep, and I remember how I just fell into my creaky dining room chair and wept when I read it.

Shaun's message said, "We're going to the Philippines. Interested?"

Compassion works in countries all over the world. The trip could have been to anywhere. They didn't know my story. But God did. The great Redeemer was redeeming my story. I was going to get to see the country my mother knew so well. I'd glimpse her culture and see sights she saw. One more rare connection to the woman I always longed to know.

He redeems.

But He still wasn't done.

A few weeks before the trip, I was up far too late wrapping up a blog post as I sat snuggled under my favorite thick blanket on my couch. Then a Facebook message popped up.

"Hi! My name is Esther Sandee. I'm one of your cousins from the Philippines . . ."

Esther Sandee? I'd heard that name before. We exchanged a few airmail letters when I was in elementary school. How did she find me? Why was she even looking?

It dawned on me: I hadn't been forgotten. My brother and

I had never been forgotten. All those years we wondered about them, they had wondered about us too.

More tears and messages back and forth. I told her I'd be in Manila in a few weeks, and she replied, "You will?! We'll come meet you."

I never could have dreamed . . .

Oh, how He redeems.

————————

Have you ever been so excited to arrive somewhere that when you walk up to the baggage claim you start to cry?

Yeah, probably not. I didn't expect to either.

It was the customs officer who triggered it. As she stamped my passport, she looked at me closely and said, "You're half Filipino, aren't you?" Having grown up in South Texas, I blended in well with the predominantly Hispanic community. No one ever guessed I was anything different.

That simple question from my favorite customs officer ever was the greatest welcome she could have given me.

And so, tears at baggage claim.

Less than twenty-four hours later, the flood of emotion and ugly crying hit the next level. It was Memorial Day 2011. I cried the first time I met my precious Compassion sponsor child, Maricor, and I cried a second time when our bus pulled back up to our hotel and I saw a group of people gathered at the front window. Watching. Waiting. And I knew. It was my family.

He redeems.

I raced off the bus into the hotel and the arms of my mother's sisters, brothers, nieces, and nephews. Eighteen of them!

Some had traveled more than twenty-four hours just to be there to meet me.

For the first time in my life, I was surrounded by women who looked like me. They were in tears to finally meet the daughter of the sister they missed so deeply, and I was in tears to be embraced by the beloved siblings of the mother I never knew. I cannot adequately express what that moment meant to me.

After a whirlwind of greetings, hugs, tears, and wonderfulness, I turned around to see my Compassion team, Shaun, Tsh, Emily, Stephanie, Lindsey, Patricia, Keely, and Bri—people I'd met less than a day before as we boarded the plane—all ugly crying right along with me.

It meant so much to me that I wasn't experiencing this moment alone. That at some level they understood how this very moment brought a level of completion to my story.

Oh, how He redeems.

———

Maybe your story is similar to mine, with parents who weren't there. Maybe yours didn't die. Maybe they left. Maybe they stayed but didn't care. Or maybe you lost a son or daughter, a brother or sister, a spouse. Maybe you're longing for a child. Maybe you lost your hope, your faith. Maybe you lost your job or your ability to dream. Maybe your story holds more heartache than most can imagine.

Maybe words have pierced you. Maybe there were fists. Maybe you disappointed yourself and others.

Or maybe you don't think you have a story, but you wish you did. Your life has been fine and good, and you wish you felt as if you needed Jesus just a little more. You wish you could trace His footsteps in your perfectly tended life. Maybe you're thankful, but you're desperate for something more. Just wait. Your story isn't over.

My story can never end the way I always wished it would, but I cherish every high and low. God is the master of the plot twist, the shocking moment of revelation when you look back and see exactly how He took all the things and worked them together for good (Rom. 8:28).

I never could have imagined how my story would end, but He conducted me through every high and low and produced a symphony from my sorrow.

I love these lyrics from singer-songwriter Christa Wells, in her song "Thousand Things":

You're gonna cry yourself to sleep,
You're gonna soak the pillow for many weeks,
You're gonna cry,
Why? Why me?

But in spite of the ache that doesn't go away,
You'll be sharing your story one rainy day,
And at the next table, somebody catches your
     words,
He hears a truth that he's never heard.

He takes it back to the marriage he'd given up on,
Hands it down to his daughter who writes it into
     song.
You didn't know . . .

A thousand things are happening in this one
*   thing,*
Like a thousand fields nourished by a single drop
*   of rain,*
So honey, wrap yourself in promise,
While you wait the morning light.

A thousand things are happening tonight.

What does all this have to do with mornings? Oh, just everything.

Stories are lived day by day. How we start matters. Our day-in and day-out choices are the pieces that build the mosaic of our lives. And while they don't always seem important or beautiful up close, when we put them all together and step back, we can see the masterpiece unfolding.

I love looking back on those hard, early days of motherhood when my inadequacy and ignorance pushed me every morning to the feet of Jesus. Following Him day by day led me to that redemptive moment in my life. It was that very morning habit that helped me start the blog I was unqualified to write, that built a ministry I was unequipped to lead, that put me on a Compassion trip that "just happened" to be to the Philippines. God orchestrated it. I simply followed each step.

And you? What is the story He longs to redeem in your life? What is the open loop that He wants to bring full circle?

The only way to know is to follow Him step by step. How we start affects how we finish. How we start shapes our journey and outlines our lives. And who we start with makes all the difference.

The beautiful thing is that every day can be a fresh start. God has a purpose for your life. You are made for His glory and the good of those around you. By ourselves, we cannot help, heal, or bring hope. He can.

All we need to do is follow. Morning by morning.

two

Do Our Mornings Matter?

Imagine I asked two people to run a mile, and each of them asked me why. I would probably get drastically different responses if I told one, "I heard it might be good for your health," and I told the other, "There's a bear chasing you, and the only safe spot is a mile away." Our motivation, our *why*, can make or break our results.

Maybe you chose this book because you've heard it's a good idea to have a morning routine. Or maybe you're reading because, like me, you've reached the end of your rope, and you're desperate for a change. Your why will deeply influence what you get out of our time together. I want you to think through the reasons you decided to read this book, but I also want to offer a why for you to consider:

Your mornings and how you live each day matter more deeply than you could imagine.

You might be thinking, *I'm not a brain surgeon or a superhero. I'm just a student, mother, office worker, teacher . . .* You can fill in the blank with whatever you like, but as you're about to see, your life, your years, your days—all of it matters more than you may realize.

The Gauntlet of Fire

When my kids were little, I referred to the grocery store check-out line as the "gauntlet of fire."

I imagined the brainstorming sessions for the design of the checkout aisle going something like this:

"I know! Let's make the aisles as narrow as possible so as people are unloading the groceries at one end, the children can sneak past the cart and wreak havoc just beyond their grasp."

"Brilliant! And let's put the toilet-shaped candy complete with a choking-hazard lollipop plunger right at the eye level of a two-year-old."

"These are only temporary trials. We'll make this a true gauntlet of fire by placing racks of magazines filled with questionable journalism and even more questionable clothing choices right where elementary-aged children can read the article titles and ask unbelievably awkward questions while customers are paying so they won't notice how much we are charging."

"Your genius is too much. We are not worthy. Mwah, ha ha ha!"

I've been told I overdramatize. Whatever.

But have you noticed the magazines in the gauntlet-of-fire

checkout lines? Aside from the apparent fabric shortage among celebrities, I've noticed that there are always at least two kinds of magazines: ones for teen girls and ones for grown women.

The ones for girls typically have titles like these:

- "Copy This Singer's Latest Fashion Statement!"
- "Learn to Style Your Hair Like Your Favorite Movie Star!"
- "Check Out How Cute This Famous Teen Couple Is!"

(And whatever the title, there are always, always exclamation points.)

But the magazines for women tend to have titles like these:

- "10 Models Who Are Ugly Without Makeup"
- "The Celebrity Couple Whose Marriage Is Over"
- "Find Out Which Actress Threw a Fit on Set"

Do you see the difference? From encouraging to destructive. What happens along our journey of life to transition us from dreaming to tearing down?

We lose hope. When we lose hope, we settle. When we settle, the only way to lift ourselves up is to tear others down.

How do we get off the hamster wheel and revive our hope? Our self-esteem, our hope needs to be centered on something more secure. Something unchanging. Someone unchanging.

What if we still believed, no matter our age, that we could be beautiful? What if we still believed we could feel smart or healthy or full of energy? What if we still believed we could change the world? What if we still believed that anything is possible?

How Do We Revive Hope?

We *can* change our thinking and believe again in a life filled with hope and the possibility of good things to come.

Let's start by looking at the definition of *possible*: "able to be done; within the power or capacity of someone or something."[1]

Scripture says, "With God, all things are possible" (Matt. 19:26).

Bingo!

If we want to revive possibility, restore hope, and believe we can still change and grow, we need to be *with* God, be renewed inwardly by Him day after day (2 Cor. 4:16). We need to start each morning with the One who makes even the impossible—possible.

You may have heard this before: Start your day with a "quiet time." Read your Bible. Pray. Maybe you've been able to do it for a while, but life always seems to get in the way. You know you "need" to do it. You might even carry guilt about all the times you've tried and failed.

But just as we know we "need" to eat more kale, sleep eight hours, and floss every single day, knowing we need to do something and actually doing it are two very different things. It's a little like knowing we need to be able to read and actually learning to read. We learn lessons and build habits along the way. I'll share more about those lessons and habits later, but right now my hope is that this book will ignite an undeniable sense of purpose within you. That every morning will feel like Christmas morning because you see the hope and possibility in each new day. That you believe you can live an exceptional life *with* God.

One in a Schmoozle

You were made to live an exceptional life. It sounds like a platitude, but it's a fact. Your life matters, and God created you unlike anyone else. Let me show you.

According to the *Wall Street Journal* bestseller *Strengths Finder 2.0* and the folks at Gallup—who have surveyed literally millions of people around the world—any one person can have thirty-four strengths. And the order in which they have them is crucial to how they use them and influence others. Did you know that the odds of any two people having the same top five strengths are 1 in 275,000? That means there probably isn't anyone like you in your town. The odds of anyone else having the same top five in the same *order* as you is 1 in 33.4 million. That means there probably isn't anyone like you in your state.[2]

The odds of anyone having all thirty-four in the same order as you is 1 in 3 x 10^{38}. That means three times a number that has thirty-eight zeroes behind it. I don't even know a name for a number that big.[3]

Let's call it a "schmoozle."

Frankly, I find the magnitude of that number a bit hard to wrap my little brain around, so I did a little research to help me grasp it. According to the Population Reference Bureau, from the beginning of time until now, there have been about 100 billion people.[4] And according to many scientists, the earth is past its midlife. Meaning, it likely won't be able to support human life for longer than it already has. (Please note, this is not a statement on the return of Christ or the creation of the world or anything fancy schmancy like that. It's simply for numerical demonstration.)

So if there have been 100 billion people on the earth, and we are past our midlife, there might only be another 100 billion. Now let's factor in population growth trends, adding in another 800 billion for fun. That gives a very generous estimate that there will never be more than about a trillion people who will exist on planet earth.

Do you know how many zeroes a schmoozle has? Thirty-eight.

Do you know how many zeroes a trillion has? Twelve.

Even a number as massive as a trillion is still a tiny fraction of a number with thirty-eight zeroes.

"Kat? What in the world are you trying to say? What do all these numbers have to do with my mornings?"

What I'm saying is that in all of human history—past, present, and future—considering every person who has ever lived and every person yet to live, there never has been and there never will be anyone like you. You are completely, incomprehensibly, and intentionally unique.

God has written the greatest story ever told. And He has given you a storyline in this epic of human history. There is a specific call on your life, there is a role for you to play—one no one else can fulfill.

No one else can influence your family as you can. No one else can impact your friends and coworkers as you can. No one else has your history, your perspective, your skills, and your talents.

He created you, and no one else, to make a particular imprint on the history of the world.

You may feel as though everyone else on earth is more qualified, more impressive, or more talented. But the truth is, we need *you*. No one can take your place. No one is better at you . . . than you.

Behind the Scenes of an Exceptional Life

What were you doing when you were sixteen years old?

If you were anything like me, the answer is . . . not very much. At least, not compared to Jessica Watson who, at the age of sixteen, completed a solo, nonstop, unassisted circumnavigation of the globe . . . in a little thirty-four-foot sailboat.

At sixteen years of age, she sailed 23,000 nautical miles. She was alone for 210 days. Her boat was knocked down (hit by waves so that it was turned completely upside down) six times, and she often found herself and her little boat in raging storms with waves four stories high.

Alone. And not just alone but thousands of miles from any other human beings.

Sixteen.

Then there's Katie Davis. She was a homecoming queen, valedictorian, and all-around average American girl, when she developed a love for the people of Uganda. At the age of nineteen, she moved around the world, began an organization that helps hundreds of children, and started the process of adopting thirteen girls.

On the other end of the spectrum is Dick Hoyt. His son Rick was unable to walk or talk, and doctors said he should be institutionalized. But Dick Hoyt and his wife had other plans. They found a computer system that helped Rick type through eye movements. One day, Rick told his father that he wanted to compete in a 5K. So Mr. Hoyt, never having raced in his life, rigged his son's wheelchair and pushed him for 3.1 miles. Racing breathed life into Rick, and he and his father continued to compete. They have completed hundreds of races including 5Ks, triathlons, and several Ironman races. At seventy-three years old, Mr. Hoyt pulls his full-grown 140-pound son in a raft for the 2.4-mile swim, carries him on his bike for the 112-mile ride, and pushes him in a wheelchair for the 26.2-mile run.

What do you think you'll be doing at seventy-three?

Stories of exceptional people inspire me to no end. What am I capable of? What are my limits? What grand, daring adventure can I pursue that stretches and tests the very limits of my physical and mental endurance?

And then one of my kids interrupts my reverie: "Mom, what's for dinner?" I promptly fall into a heap, saying, "I just don't know! Why do you people need to eat every single day? I can't handle cooking another meal!"

At that point I realize that the wild, faithful pursuit of big adventures is so much more glamorous than the wild, faithful pursuit of the everyday. But it's in the middle of the mundane that we lay the foundation for our greatest adventures.

I don't know about you, but my life isn't very full of big adventures right now. It is full of cooking, cleaning, helping with homework, picking up socks, and myriad monotonous tasks.

Maybe your life is similar. So how do we live wildly, bravely, and exceptionally in the midst of the ordinary? In the midst of the dinners that need to be cooked, the work needing to be done, and the bills that need to be paid?

We do it by living with wild, exceptional excellence in the small things, remembering that the habits we foster and the character we build along the way are the heart of our greatest triumphs.

Jessica didn't buy a sailboat one weekend and say, "See ya!" to her mom and dad.

Kate didn't grab a last-minute flight to Uganda with name tags for thirteen kids.

The Hoyts didn't attend a triathlon and just jump in on the fun.

There's a backstory. Practicing and packing. Preparing and praying. Failing and trying again. And again. And again. They invested countless hours in boring moments no one saw. The exceptional life is the tip of the iceberg. It's easy to look at people we admire and think that they simply have it all together or that they have something we don't. In reality, they simply try and try again. Their success is built on the foundation of faithfulness.

Mother Teresa is a beautiful example of this truth. She undoubtedly lived an exceptional life, but it wasn't marked by any one big thing she did. We know her because of her wild obedience to the small things. The lepers. The children. The poor. The people everyone else saw but walked right by.

Small, simple things make the big things possible. So regardless of your season or situation, don't be afraid to dream big and start now. Live with wild, exceptional excellence in the small things; they are the very foundation of grand adventures.

You see, living an exceptional life isn't just an opportunity that comes along once in a lifetime. It's an invitation that awaits us every single day. Every single morning.

Living Exceptional Days

It's amazing what can happen in the course of a day:

- Friends become husband and wife.
- Babies are welcomed into the world.
- Someone once unemployed gets a new job.
- An author's book is finally published.
- A daughter speaks words of forgiveness to her mother.
- A woman sits down on a bus and ignites a civil rights movement.
- Troops storm the beaches of Normandy and redirect the course of history.
- Jessica Watson enters Sydney Harbor as the youngest person to ever sail around the globe.

But remember: while all these events mark a sudden and official shift in one day, what goes uncelebrated are the years and years of purpose and focus that made those monumental days possible.

A published book is the result of endless study, writing, and editing.

A new job comes only after years of education, résumé writing, and job interviews.

When Rosa Parks got on that bus, her history of involvement in the Montgomery NAACP and her training in nonviolent resistance at the Highlander Folk School had prepared her for that moment and all the moments that followed.

Troops practiced the invasion of Normandy for months and months prior to June 6, 1944.

Jessica dedicated years of her life, day after day, to get across her finish line.

Anything is possible in the course of one day, but it is also true that anything is possible when we line up the dominoes day after day—when we build the habits, pray the prayers, and trust in a God who makes dry bones come alive (Ezek. 37:5).

I don't know about you, but I want to live as if every day is a big day and start each day so that I lay the dominoes for greater things to come.

When Life Interrupts Our Attempts to Live Exceptionally

But some days . . . are just hard.

It was a terrible, horrible, no good, very bad day, and I was sure I was a terrible, horrible, no good, very bad wife, mom, friend, human being, and general occupier of space on planet earth.

But at least I wasn't prone to drama.

I sat in my minivan, in my garage, in July, in Texas, having a pity party. The sweat and the tears streamed down my face, and I mentally calculated the cost of all the therapy everyone in my life was going to need after interacting with me that day.

I'd been grumpy, rude, and impatient.

I felt exhausted, unfocused, and overwhelmed.

And if I was honest, it wasn't just that day. It was one of many, and I was on a very slippery slope. I needed something to change. I felt dry, empty, and hopeless. Little did I know that this low point was the beginning of a season of coming alive again.

Dry Bones?

It's one of the craziest stories in the Bible. And by crazy, I mean completely weird and illogical. You're probably going to think I'm insane for even telling it. Cray-zee.

A prophet named Ezekiel was walking and talking with God one day, and God took him to a valley filled with dried-up bones. Ezekiel stood overlooking the dry, empty, hopeless valley, and God said to him, "Can these bones live?"

It's a good thing I'm not Ezekiel.

My reply would have been more like, "Um. I don't know, maybe . . . okay . . . yes, but can we please *not* do that? Because . . . creepy."

Thankfully, for humanity and Sunday school classes everywhere, Ezekiel was a tad more spiritual than me.

"Sovereign LORD, you alone know" (Ezek. 37:1–3).

Well played.

As a result of Ezekiel's willingness to follow God, listen, and obey, God did the miraculous through him. God told Ezekiel to speak to the valley, to say, "You will come to life!" And it did. The bones rattled together, they put on flesh, they rose up and stood as an army—ready to do as God commanded. From death to life. From dry, empty, and hopeless—the ultimate defeat—to a living, breathing army.

When Everything Changed

Maybe you feel a little dry and defeated. Maybe you need to see God perform a miracle in the valley of your life. I know I did.

As I sat in my garage, in tears, I asked God to speak to my dry, empty, and hopeless heart. I needed Him to make me come alive again—but how?

In this season of life, I had three small children. My customary alarm clock was the impact of one of the aforementioned small people launching themselves onto my bed, crawling up to my face, and whisper-yelling, *"Mommy! Are you awake? Can I have Cheerios? Can I watch cartoons? Why are your eyes closed? Mommy? Mommy!"*

I consistently woke up playing defense, feeling out of sync, and trying to catch up for the rest of the day. And it never worked.

I was giving out of my own emptiness. And I had nothing.

I needed to see the hope in my days. What I saw before me was a valley of diaper changes, a dusty college degree, and not much hope. I needed to see more than a valley of bones. I needed to stand with God and trust in Him to speak life to my days. I needed to come alive, and I couldn't do that alone.

No matter how long Ezekiel spoke to that valley, no matter what he said or how hard he tried, nothing would have changed without the power of God.

All my striving and straining each day was hopeless if I wasn't standing with God, speaking His words, and believing that what He saw in my valley was greater than what I saw.

Even if it was just waking up five minutes earlier, I wanted to stand with God, overlooking my day and speaking His truth into those dry and empty places.

I wanted to start my day with purpose. To remember why I do what I do, and fill my tank so I could serve and love others out of the overflow in me.

So I did the unthinkable. I set my alarm.

I spent some quiet time reading my Bible, planning my day, and going for a run. Some days I skipped the run and did one jumping jack. Yes, one jumping jack. Progress—not perfection, people.

I rewarded myself by lighting a pretty candle, having a carafe of hot coffee ready, and playing my morning music playlist.

I started getting excited about getting up early. Who does that?

Me, apparently.

Then I started getting excited about going to bed early. I didn't want to be exhausted in the morning. I started getting more rest, more exercise, and more vision for my life. My streak of terrible, horrible, no good, very bad days slowed to a trickle.

Not Too Far Gone

What I love about Ezekiel's story is that God didn't just do it Himself and make Ezekiel a spectator of His awesomeness, which would have been perfectly fine. Instead, He allowed Ezekiel to be a part of this crazy miracle. God spoke *through* him.

Do areas in your life feel like dry bones? Your spiritual life? Your marriage? Your relationship with your family or your children? Your career? Your self-esteem?

I wish I could jump right out of this book, take your hands, do a crazy dance, and share a fraction of the hope I feel in Christ. With Him *all* things are possible. *All* things.

Your marriage is not too far gone.
Your health is not too far gone.
Your life is not too far gone.
Even death is not beyond His mighty power.

But the wonder and hope of Christ go far beyond our rescuing and saving. Following Jesus means we can be used, through Him, to be world changers, life givers, and relationship restorers. Not in our own power or for our own glory, but in Him, through Him, and by Him we get to be a part of the greatest stories ever told.

You have everything you need. Now is the time to start. He is waiting for you to rise up. He'll do all the miracle stuff; He just asks that you hope and follow and speak His words to the valley.

Musical Montage

My favorite part of almost every movie is what I call the musical montage. It usually starts with the main character realizing the need for change and taking drastic action.

The alarm clock rings at o'dark-thirty. Heart-thumping theme music pounds as the character bolts out of bed, drinks raw eggs, and runs a bajillion miles in the dark wearing a stylish hoodie, greeting the sunrise in a triumphant mountaintop moment.

I don't know about you, but there is nothing in me that naturally *wants* to wake up at o'dark-thirty, drink raw eggs, or run a bajillion (or any) miles.

So why do those characters do it?

Because they have decided that *who* they are becoming is more important than *what* they have to do to get there. They realize that their capacity, time, willpower, and focus are the strongest first thing in the day, before all the craziness of life invades.

Let's be honest, I still have less-than-stellar days sometimes, but they are fewer and further apart. And in between have been days I could never have even dreamed of.

This small, intentional act of starting each day with Jesus has been the catalyst for incredible things in my life, from blogging and e-books to traveling around the world and meeting my family for the first time.

Your Mornings Matter

My morning routine has been a retreat; a filling station; an energizing, envisioning, wonderfully infectious habit that has brought peace, calm, and order to so many other areas of my life.

It started small, messy, and (honestly) lazy. Sometimes I would fall asleep during my morning routine. Sometimes I still do. It isn't always perfect, but it is . . . always.

I've learned to wake up *for* my life instead of just *to* my life. It has become a habit. It's my default. When things get out of control and crazy, my morning time with God is what I always come back to. My morning routine feels as if I'm crawling into the lap of my heavenly Father and He's wrapping His arms around me, and all seems right with the world. It's where He reminds me who I am, whose I am, and what I'm called to do. Then we make a plan to get it done. I'm filled up to give.

I can face my day, not in my own power and organization, but in His.

Your morning routine can be your daily reset button. As Anne of Green Gables said, "Isn't it nice to think that tomorrow is a new day with no mistakes in it yet?"[5]

Taking the time to sit and savor all the possibility wrapped up in the next twenty-four hours is refreshing, inspiring, and invigorating. The One who, with a simple whisper to your heart, can make all right with the world, waits ever so patiently for you each morning. He knows you. He wants you. He remembers your biggest dreams, your secret hopes, and your desperate prayers. He paid a great price to meet you in your darkest hour, to give you the greatest gift.

He is my greatest gift, the source of my hope and security. With Him, every single day, all things are possible.

God Holds Our Possibilities

Think about it. If I believe God created me with a specific purpose and plan for my life, then He must have a purpose and plan for my year. If He has a purpose and plan for my year, He has a purpose and plan for my days. That means He has a purpose and plan for *today*. And if my all-knowing, all-powerful, loving God has a plan for my day, why wouldn't I want to be a part of it?

He created me and understands my deepest needs. He knows the most powerful ways I can be used to bring glory to Him and bring hope and healing to others. He knows exactly how I can have the greatest impact with my life, with every single day.

How could checking e-mail, Facebook, or Instagram compare with checking in with the God of the universe who has an agenda for my day that is a perfect fit for me?

Every morning we have the choice to trudge through the day without vision or direction, feeling purposeless and overwhelmed. Or we can connect with God, glimpse His directions for our lives, understand who we can influence, and discern how we can grow and ways we can bring Him glory today.

When we think about it that way, why would we want to start our mornings any other way?

Every Day Is a Big Day

We wake up early when we have a big day. Maybe it's the first day of school or a holiday. Maybe we're catching a vacation flight, or we're eager for Christmas morning. Maybe it's our first day of work or our wedding day.

Whatever the occasion, we wake up early when something important is happening. What if every day felt important? What if every day felt as if it was bursting with meaning and hope?

It is, it should, and it can.

As long as we are alive, we have room to grow. There is always hope, possibility, and another peak to climb.

So if you find yourself at a fork in the road, choose the climb.

Cue your musical montage.

three

Are You Ready?

Every year my family takes a huge trip. We're like the Griswolds on steroids. If we spend fewer than fifty hours in the car, hit fewer than five different states, and log fewer than three thousand miles, we pretty much consider it a trip to the grocery store.

Over the past five years we've visited thirty US states and logged hundreds of hours in the car. By the time you read these words, we'll have been to all but six of the lower forty-eight states.

While my husband plans our trips, I do all the packing for the kids, gather the snacks, and come up with the entertainment. (We're big on audiobooks and books.) Before we head out on our epic adventures, we always do one important thing: we evaluate. For the trip to be successful, we have to be aware of our kids' personalities and our own personalities and limits, and then we make a plan based on that.

We know that our oldest teen, Anna, thrives when she has some alone time and a space to retreat to. So we give her the far back seat all to herself. She can play games with her siblings if she wants, but she can also be left alone if that's what she needs. We know our son Jackson and daughter Alli want to be in the center of it all—to listen in on Mom and Dad's conversations, play games with one another, and have easy access to our snacks. Jimmy loves to drive. So far, on our trips he has driven every single mile. I much prefer to sit and read, write, or pass endless snacks back to the kids.

We also know what snacks people like and how exactly to organize our things in the car for maximum tidiness (I can't stand a messy car on a road trip, though it always descends into chaos at some point) and to make it as easy as possible to access what we need.

We know that if there is a sign with historical writing on it, Jimmy will read it in its entirety, and the kids are content to entertain themselves while he reads. (The kids and I may have napped on benches at the Smithsonian.) Jimmy knows that I *hate* heights—especially when my kids are with me. So he goes the speed limit, has two hands on the wheel, and doesn't tell me he's enjoying the view when we are on "scenic drives." If we didn't know these things about ourselves, our road trips would be disastrous.

There is so much power in awareness—in knowing yourself and those around you.

Building a morning habit is something like going on a long road trip. You're in it for the long haul, so you need to know yourself. You need to accommodate your personality, preferences, and passions. In this chapter, we're going to do some fun self-discovery. We are going to delve into the morning myths that hold us back and understand how personalities, time, and seasons affect our mornings.

Understanding You

One of our great responsibilities in life is to discover who we are, where we thrive, and what we offer that no one else can. What are those unique things God wove into us that need to be tended to bloom? What are our strengths and weaknesses? In what situations do we thrive, and in what situations do we struggle? What makes us come alive?

It might feel a little narcissistic to spend time truly studying yourself, but doing it can bring you so much clarity and peace.

I've learned that I'm something called an *ambivert*. It's someone who is right in the middle of being an extrovert and introvert. I love people and can be really energized by social situations but I also very much need to step away afterward and process all the input and interaction. Learning this about myself explained so many situations when I hit a boiling point and felt frustrated with everyone around me. I've now learned to recognize when I'm getting overloaded; I pull away to spend some time alone even if the extrovert part of me really wants to continue to socialize. It's a simple thing, but it has saved me so much heartache.

What about you? Do you know what drains you and what fills you? How do you best process your emotions? What helps you focus as you pray or read the Word?

How Does This Help with Mornings?

There are millions of ways to build a morning routine using the endless options for Bible study, prayer, planning, exercise, and orchestrating our time. But just as we wouldn't walk into a clothing store and buy an outfit without knowing our size and fit, we can't expect to adopt a routine for our mornings without knowing if it's a good match for our time, season, and heart.

So many new habits fail because we hear about something that worked well for someone else and we jump on the bandwagon—no questions asked. We forget that what might work for one person won't work for another. Also, what might work in one season of your life might not work in another season of your life. We must take stock of our current situation and learn as much as we can about what works for us now—so we don't try to force pieces together that don't fit.

We can't adopt a morning routine just because it works for our favorite celebrity or because it worked for us back in high school. Things change. People change. So we're going to take the time to do a simple self-assessment to give our new habits the best opportunity to stick.

When We Know Better, We Do Better

Maybe you struggle with waking up. If so, then determine whether it's because you're not getting enough sleep or because you need a more pleasant alarm—one that's kinder than the blaring, million-decibel alarm that immediately puts you in a state of panic.

Does music move you deeply? Then consider starting your day with a worship song, structuring your morning in a more personal and powerful way.

Maybe you're a visual person, and the best way to get your energy flowing and your mind focused on God would be to start your morning by drawing or writing out scriptures.

If you enjoy making new connections in Scripture then the

best way for you to begin your day might be to read a passage and then take notes as you study all the cross-references.

Or you might be a pen-and-paper girl, but you also need the order of a digital planning system because the thought of losing a paper planner stresses you out.

Or perhaps fitness is part of your morning routine. In the area of fitness, knowing yourself is crucial because there are so many experts who will tell you what they think is the best thing to do. And because we often feel so intimidated by fitness experts, and all the things we don't understand about exercise and nutrition, we just follow along blindly, not realizing that we are sabotaging our own efforts.

For example, I cannot handle group fitness. I love solitary exercise, whether that's working out at the gym or going for a nice long run—alone. I enjoy the opportunity to think and move at my own pace. I suppose this is where my introvert half comes in. I only like exercising with others when it's in the form of a game or competition of some sort.

We can waste so much time trying to fit a square peg of what is popular or seems like the "right way" into the round hole of what actually works for us. Instead, let's bypass all that trial and error and take a shortcut to our ideal morning routine.

Personal Inventory

To get started, let's take a personal inventory so we understand our starting point and our resources for the journey toward a great morning routine. To determine what will work best for you, let's consider four things:

1. Season and Situation

In some seasons of life, we can easily start or grow a morning routine. In others, survival is hard enough, and thinking about adding anything feels overwhelming—yet it's in those hard seasons when we need God, a plan, and good health the most. Understanding the pressures and priorities of the season you are in will allow you to wisely incorporate a life-giving routine into your day.

Season

What season are you in? Just as the world has seasons for growing, shedding, resting, and blooming, we also have seasons where our needs differ. Do you have a newborn? Did you just move, start a new job, start school, or lose a loved one? Maybe this is a season for grace and a slow pace. A three-minute morning with very gradual incremental changes might be healthiest for you right now.

Did your kids just start school or head off to college? Maybe you just finished college and are in a rhythm in the working world. This might be a good time to try new things and grow your morning a little more briskly.

Take a few minutes and consider whether you're in a summer, fall, winter, or spring season of life. Place a checkmark in the box beside your current season.

☐ Summer: Life feels good and warm, and you have space and time to try new things and grow.
☐ Fall: Life is full, you're super busy, and there seems to be no focus. It might be time to scale back in some areas in order to thrive.

☐ Winter: The busyness of life finally catches up, and you're worn out. Rest is the key to prospering in this season. It's about snuggling down with those people and things you hold most dear.

☐ Spring You're aching for bigger things and ready to stretch yourself and push beyond your current comfort and limits.

Situation

You might be wondering how a situation would be different from your season. Let me explain. While there might be two moms with newborns, maybe one is a single, first-time mom with a colicky baby and the other has two elementary-aged children, a husband who works from home, and the easiest newborn on the planet.

Or there might be two people who are both college students, but one is a nineteen-year-old having fun living in the dorm and taking entry-level classes. The other might be a doctoral candidate who is also working a full-time job to pay for school while raising a family.

Same seasons; different situations.

Details and circumstances matter. They influence the expectations we should and should not have of ourselves. So take some time to evaluate your season and situation. Be realistic about what you can take on now as you build your morning routine. Do you have the capacity to focus and build quickly, or should you take it slow so you don't burn out with everything else on your plate? Or perhaps it's time to prune some of the other things in your life to make room for growth.

What are the unique aspects of your current situation?

_____

_____

_____

_____

2. Time

Have you ever wondered where all your time goes? You're about to find out. This activity can be quite the eye-opener.

Just as those who want to spend their money more wisely keep a budget, and those who want to eat more healthfully keep a food journal, if we want to use our time well, there is no better place to start than a time-tracking page.

It's easy to think we don't have time to study our Bible, plan, or take care of our health, much less all three. It's easy to feel as though we barely have time to get dressed in the morning, much less add a new routine. But the simple act of tracking your time may reveal fifteen minutes of snooze-button time you could use, or time spent in the kitchen cooking when you could also be prepping lunches for the next day.

A good spring-cleaning of your schedule has the potential to reveal lovely treasures of time that can make your morning routine a simple possibility rather than a big stretch.

Take a day and track how you spend your time in fifteen- to thirty-minute increments. You can be more or less specific depending on how your day flows. For example, if you commute for ninety minutes, just write that down. Or if you exercise for fifteen minutes and shower for fifteen minutes, write down each of those.

Yes, it's a bit of a hassle to do this exercise, but it is well worth it.

When I did this for the first time, I realized that I spend two to three hours a day carpooling my children to school and activities. Wow! And I live in a small town where all our activities are less than five miles from our home.

When I realized how much time I spend driving, I started keeping Bible-verse cards to memorize in the car to use that time more effectively.

And when Jimmy saw what my schedule looked like, he realized he could help out even more and free up more of my time to write without affecting his schedule adversely. Hallelujah chorus!

Now, hear me: I'm not saying someone will step in and help if you track your time, but at the very least you'll be able to identify spots in your schedule that you can use more effectively or activities you can delegate to someone or eliminate altogether.

I also realized I'm not awesome at relaxing, so I've made it a point to work hard during work hours and then relax hard (no pseudo work—e-mail, social media, or otherwise) in the evenings and on weekends. This has been a wonderfully peace-filled change.

You might, like me, discover you waste *way* too much time randomly checking social media in the evenings, and it leaves you feeling drained and less connected than before. It is far more restful to just skip the extra social media time and take a walk or get more sleep. If you go to bed earlier, it's easier to get up earlier—a simple way to shift your schedule and have time to build a great morning routine.

"I don't have time" is one of the biggest reasons people don't exercise, plan, or spend time with God. Tracking your time will help you see how much time you actually have and how you can use it in the most life-giving way.

Here are a few questions to ask yourself before and after you track your time:

- Where am I spending most of my time?

_____

- Am I getting enough sleep?

_____

- Does any part of my daily schedule need to change?

_____

- Am I taking the time for personal refreshment?

_____

- Could any of my time be better spent?

_____

- Are there any hidden pockets of time I could use better?[1]

_____

3. Personality Type

I'm not going to lie; I love personality tests. My family even does them for fun. Just last month, after several days of travel and not a lot of sleep, my nine-year-old used his Myers-Briggs personality type to convince us he didn't need to take a nap: "Mama, Myers-Briggs says I'm like a 90 percent 'extro-vert-er' and only 10 percent 'introvert-er,' so I will get more energy being out there with everyone instead of in here alone."

Now, while most of us would prefer to figure out how *to* take a nap, knowing your personality type can be helpful for other things, like understanding how best to structure your morning routine.

For example, Sarah-Jane, a public relations specialist and mom of two, said:

> The planner in me really likes to schedule the day early—especially on the weekends when I'm home with the kids. In my plan time, I outline every hour of the day and all of our to-do lists. I also plan in fun things and unstructured time for relaxing. But, it's all planned. I feel confident going into the day knowing what to expect, and it helps me let my kids know what to expect from the day right away.
>
> On the extrovert side, I'm a part of a group of ladies who all text each other to hold ourselves accountable to getting up before our kids to spend time with Jesus. Just knowing they are expecting a text from me (typically the first one since I'm an early-morning gal) is good motivation for me to remain consistent.

But other people such as Karen H., a part-time attorney and homeschooling mom of three boys, need quite the opposite:

> As an introvert, I am pretty much always feeling behind in my day and have a higher level of stress and anxiety if I do not get time alone in the morning. Ideally, I am up at

least an hour before anyone else. Even if my kids are in the other room, it's not sufficient. I need absolute alone time; otherwise, it's so hard for me to have the emotional energy to deal with the day!

Quite honestly, you could get lost in the fascinating world of personality types and never finish this book. Since we don't want *that* to happen, here are a few suggestions:

- Start with one personality test and dive in. There are so many personality tests (see the following list) that it's easy to just take all of them and never walk away with helpful nuggets of truth. So limit yourself to one or two tests to identify your personality type and strengths.
- Take personality test results as guides, not facts. Personality tests do not define you; they simply help you understand you. We get different results in different seasons and stages of life. Let this be an ongoing process to discover how you grow and develop.
- Test the results. Don't assume that a test created decades ago can figure out the nuances of your life and experiences. Test out the results to see if they ring true for you.
- Take the test as the "healthiest version of you." Podcaster and Myers-Briggs aficionado Megan Tietz recommends answering personality tests as the healthiest version of you. Meaning that if you have a newborn and never get out or have adult conversations, you might test as a super-social extrovert when in normal, everyday life, you're more of an introvert. So as you answer questions,

think of your response in slight generalities rather than exactly how you're feeling at that moment.

Personality Test Resources

A plethora of personality tests exists, but here are a few of the most popular (listed in order of simple to complex):

Smalley/Trent Animal Personality Test

This is a great starter test. It's simple, quick, insightful, and free:[2]

www.sagestrategies.biz/documents/
FiveMinutePersonalityTestforclass.pdf

Myers-Briggs

The Myers-Briggs personality assessment is probably one of the most common type indicators. There are free versions online that are excellent. I like the 16 Personalities site. But the official version requires a fee:

www.16personalities.com
www.mbtionline.com

DISC

This is another fee-based test that is often used in the workplace. It's very in-depth and insightful:

www.discprofile.com

StrengthsFinder

StrengthsFinder is a little different because it's not a broad personality indicator but rather, as the name signifies, a strengths identifier. I really like this one because it provides a collection of information and insight different from standard personality tests:

www.gallupstrengthscenter.com

Enneagram

This one is newer to me, but I have friends who rave about it. Like most of the others, there are free versions and fee-based tests:

www.enneagramspectrum.com

www.enneagraminstitute.com

What is your unique personality? Take one of the tests listed and determine yours. Then record it here so you don't forget what it is, as I often do.

_____

_____

_____

_____

4. Drainers and Fillers

We all have things we must do every day. Some things we like, and some things we don't. While we can't necessarily change what we do, it can be helpful to recognize what brings us life and energy and what takes life and energy out of us so we can make small adjustments where possible. Let's call these drainers and fillers.

First, think through regular, daily activities—what drains you and what causes you joy. What do you get excited about, and what do you dread?

For example, I'm not a party planner. I derive no joy and feel the opposite of happy when I'm assigned to organize a holiday party It's a complete drainer. I will come. I will eat. I will party. Plan the party? Please, no.

But I love being a chaperone and hanging out with the kids on field trips. Knowing this about myself allows me to feel okay about never signing up to host a party, but instead always adding my name to the chaperone list.

How do we find our drainers and fillers? The easiest place to begin is by looking through your time-tracking list and making notes about each activity you do at least weekly.

Here are a few questions to ask yourself as you look through the list of your regular activities:

* Which activities did I look forward to?

_____

_____

* Which activities left me with more energy for the rest of my day?

_____

_____

* Which activities drained me?

_____

_____

- Which relational interactions drained me?

_____

_____

- Which relational interactions filled me?

_____

_____

- What activities do I need to make more time for?

_____

_____

- What activities should I try to delegate or delete from my schedule?

_____

_____

Take a few more minutes to think about other occasional activities that drain or fill you. And ask these questions:

- The holidays: What drains me and what fills me?

_____

_____

- Travel: What aspects of travel drain or fill me? How can I compensate?

_____

_____

• Seasons: What seasons drain or fill me most?

_____

_____

The beauty of separating regular and occasional activities is that we can spot in advance those drainers that can throw us and our morning routine off kilter, as often happens during the holidays and amid changes to our schedule.

Once you have a master list of drainers and fillers (you can always add, of course), then you can apply them to your decision-making and how you spend your time.

To bring this down to a super practical level, let's think through the potential drainers and fillers in our morning routines. I'll start with an example.

This might be the worst confession ever in a book about Bible study and _God_ time, but . . . I am terrible at sitting and praying. It is exhausting for me to focus and concentrate and sit. At some level, it drains me. But I love pacing and praying or walking and praying or driving and praying. Something about the movement with prayer allows me to focus and feel energized to pray longer.

I have also found that I journal much better in a plain spiral notebook with colorful pens. Having a really pretty bound journal stresses me out because I am afraid I'll mess it up. Consequently, I write less often and less freely in it. Your drainers and fillers can be small or large, and you can find them anywhere.

Here are some questions to ask yourself:

- What helps me wake up? What makes it easier to wake up? (For example, warm blankets on cold mornings or a coffee maker on a timer.)

_____

_____

- How do I most like to study the Bible?

_____

_____

- Do I prefer to pray in my head or out loud? Sitting or walking? Praying freely or praying scriptures?

_____

_____

- Do I like to journal? If so, what sorts of journaling tools make it fun for me? Markers, notebooks, question prompts?

_____

_____

When we know what drains us and what fills us, we can build a morning routine that's easier to stick with. Then God can truly fill us to overflowing.

What Labels Are We Misusing?

In a classic study by Robert Rosenthal and Lenore Jacobson, a group of elementary school teachers was told that a select number of their students had excelled on a test that identified them as students who would likely exceed expectations and "bloom" that year. In reality, those students scored average, compared to their classmates.

Yet in a follow-up review a year later, those exact students outperformed their peers by ten to fifteen IQ points. The sole indicator was that the teachers expected them to perform better; they mentally labeled them as superior, and those students rose to that label.[3] Labels are powerful.

It's important, therefore, to recognize the labels we give ourselves. When we say, "Well, I'd like to have a morning routine, but I'm just not a morning person," we are allowing our perspective to hold us back. Sure, some people have a tendency to prefer evenings to morning, and others have a hard time getting going in the morning. But those simple facts don't eliminate the possibility of having a life-giving morning routine.

Plenty of farmers aren't morning people, but they still have to get up, milk the cows, and feed the animals. Not all long-distance commuters are morning people, but they do what they have to do to live their lives. Not all parents are morning people, yet morning after morning they wake up to tend to the needs of their children.

Maybe you're living under a label. Maybe at one point in time, you tried to do "all the things" in the morning and burned out. You pushed yourself and got out of bed at the crack of dawn, and you were really proud of your self-discipline. Your friends told you how impressed they were. Everything clicked.

But then something happened. You got sick, your alarm

didn't go off, you had to travel. Something threw you off your game. You tumbled back to the bottom of the self-discipline mountain, and as you looked back up to see how far you'd fallen, you decided you didn't have what it took to start again. So you stopped getting up early and started telling yourself that you're not a morning person. You labeled yourself.

Or maybe it's not about mornings. Maybe you've labeled yourself as someone who isn't organized or who can't figure out how to have a quiet time or who simply doesn't have what it takes to make healthy choices. Maybe you've labeled yourself as undisciplined or lazy, lacking self-control.

The labels we give ourselves and others are powerful. Just as we encourage children to choose their words carefully with the old adage "If you don't have something nice to stay, don't say anything at all," we should choose the words we use to describe ourselves carefully.

Self-criticism is the greatest form of self-sabotage. There is a fine line between honest critique of where we have room to grow and labeling ourselves in a way that stunts our growth.

The good news is that most of the things we think are necessary to build a morning routine are really not necessary at all. You don't have to be a morning person, and you don't have to be a model of self-discipline. You don't have to be organized or full of willpower.

In fact, you're going to learn that you don't need any more discipline or self-control to have a life-giving morning routine than you do to tie your shoelaces. You're going to learn that our God is the God of the impossible and, when we walk with Him day by day, those labels fall right off.

Only wear the labels God gives you. All others hold you back.

One day after church my daughter came out of Sunday school covered in return-address labels. I cried.

True, I do have a deep love of office supplies, but that's not why I teared up. Apparently the kids spent time praying that morning, asking God if there were any encouragements they could give one another. Each child got a sheet of labels and a Sharpie. They prayed and then walked around, placing labels on one another:

Full of kindness

Child of God

A worshipper

Thoughtful

Loving

A leader

Good friend

Loved by Jesus

Courageous

I saw one child in particular who by the world's standards had a severe disability. The label on his chest read, "God's masterpiece. Nothing missing. Nothing broken."

Friend, in Christ, nothing is missing, and nothing about you is broken. Whatever the labels are that hold you down, send them back to the pit where they came from. It's time to replace them with God's labels.

Here are a few labels He's given us:

- In Christ, we are set free: "Because through Christ Jesus the law of the Spirit who gives life has set you free from the law of sin and death" (Rom. 8:2).
- In Christ, we are new: "Therefore, if anyone is in Christ, the new creation has come: The old has gone, the new is here!" (2 Cor. 5:17).
- In Christ, we are complete: "In Christ you have been brought to fullness. He is the head over every power and authority" (Col. 2:10).
- In Christ, we have hope: "I pray that the eyes of your heart may be enlightened in order that you may know the hope to which he has called you, the riches of his glorious inheritance in his holy people" (Eph. 1:18).

Will you take a few minutes right now to identify the labels you're wearing that might be holding you down? Pray and ask God what He says about you. What are the labels He has given you or wants to give you if you'll only let go of those lesser ones?

_____

_____

_____

_____

Grace Over Perfection?

How much do you value perfection versus progress? It's an obstacle I often see women face when shaping a morning routine in line with their deepest values. Pursuing God, living intentionally, and taking care of our health are all deeply important to us, and we don't want to fall short. But if our goal is perfection, we are setting ourselves up for discouragement and even failure.

The pursuit of perfection is often the very thing that keeps us from progress. By focusing on all-or-nothing success, anything short of perfection is considered failure. And with each perceived failure, perseverance becomes more difficult. *Perfect* is a mirage that is always just out of reach, leaving us more desperate than when we started.

So what can we focus on instead of perfection?

You'll find few examples in Scripture of anyone waiting until they were perfect to act. In fact, most moved before they felt ready—before things seemed to make sense. They stepped out in faith. My challenge to you is to step out in faith too. Believe that God can handle your baby steps. That He can turn your fish and loaves into something so much greater than you could ever dream up on your own.

God doesn't need our perfect. He already is perfect. He just wants our yes. He just wants us to step out in faith to follow Him even if what we are doing looks pathetic, as it did for David when he fought a giant while armed with only a small stone (1 Sam. 17), or ridiculous, as it did to the Israelites marching around Jericho (Josh. 6), or scary, as it did to Esther (Est. 4).

Our step of faith may be small, but God says He can move mountains with faith the size of a mustard seed.

The key here is grace. Grace for mistakes. Grace for failure. Grace for days when we just don't want to get out of bed.

It's easy when building a habit to think we need *willpower*.

And *self-discipline*. And *hard work. Just try harder!* But we also need a massive amount of grace. Not excuses, but grace. See, the beauty of what we've learned so far is that we don't need all that much willpower, self-discipline, or hard work. We really just need a simple plan and the flexibility to figure out what works for us.

Grace comes in when life doesn't follow our plan. When we get sick, when we're traveling, or we just don't want to, and we don't. We don't get up. We don't read. We don't pray. We don't plan anything except to eat a box of doughnuts.

And then comes the guilt.

Now, guilt can be a good thing. It's a trigger to remind us that we aren't doing what we value. But triggers are temporary. They exist to remind but not to remain.

If we don't follow guilt with grace, we give up, we get stuck, we wallow, and it leads to a downward spiral. So why, then, is grace so hard in the face of guilt? Somehow it feels wrong. It feels as if we should be hard on ourselves, as if we don't deserve grace. As if grace is unnatural.

That's because it is. It is supernatural. It is what God wants to give us. The more we practice receiving grace, the more freedom we have to walk in relationship with God.

We can follow the formula: guilt + grace = growth. Let's allow our guilt to trigger a reminder that we are not living the way we value and then accept the grace that God offers to us so we can move forward in freedom (as opposed to giving up). Then we experience true growth.

Not only is grace a biblical principle, it's also scientifically proven to move you forward and to actually help you make better decisions. In 2007, the now famous "Doughnut Study" was conducted at Duke University. Researchers requested that health-conscious participants eat a doughnut in the first part of the study. Once they completed that task, participants were put in a room with candy and told they could eat as much as they liked. Half the people were told to give themselves some grace—that eating the doughnut benefited research and they shouldn't feel bad about it. The other half of the group were given no such message.

As a result, the group given no message of grace, or "self-compassion" as the study calls it, ate more than 50 percent more candy than the "grace group." This study shows that when we choose to give ourselves grace, we go on to make remarkably better choices toward our goals.[4]

So instead of trying to have a perfect habit each day, give yourself grace when you need to adjust for a difficult season. Give yourself grace if your prayer time isn't as long as you want it to be. You'll get there. Just keep going. Being frustrated with yourself when you fall short does nothing to get you where you want to go.

True, this study didn't dive into biblical grace. But the next logical step is to reflect on how we respond, not only to self-grace but also to what happens when we accept the grace God offers us each day. When we remember that He isn't standing at the finish line awaiting our triumphant victory or harshly judging us for every failure, and when we choose to cling to 2 Corinthians 12:9, we can move forward in His grace and strength: "He said to me, 'My grace is sufficient for you, for my power is made perfect in weakness.' Therefore I will boast all the more gladly about my weaknesses, so that Christ's power may rest on me."

Of course, this isn't a free pass to not try or to be lazy. This is simply an opportunity to acknowledge our current state and give God the glory for taking the next step.

I love how Beth Moore has described grace: "Grace treats us like we already are what we fear we'll never become."[5] Choose grace over perfection, and allow the slow, steady steps of progress to motivate you to be all God dreamed for you.

Scripture says God knit you together in your mother's womb (Ps. 139:13). Have you ever knit or watched someone transform a ball of yarn into a treasured keepsake? Knitting is not an instant process. It takes time, focus, and care. God carefully crafted you to do great things with your days. It's worth our time to investigate our strengths, weaknesses, and resources. From this foundation of knowledge and choosing grace over perfection, we can confidently build a morning routine that can carry us through any storm and season.

four

Laying the Foundation for Your Morning Routine

Now that we've talked about the importance of each day and spent time examining when and how to make space for a growing morning routine, I'd like to introduce you to some of the core concepts of Hello Mornings and how they can help you shape a foundational habit.

You'll remember from the first chapter that Hello Mornings started with a short twenty-five-page e-book I wrote called *Maximize Your Mornings*, and it grew into a movement. The first online accountability group formed back in August 2010, and it has grown to include thousands of women in countries around the world, with hundreds of volunteer group leaders. While you got the basics back in chapter 1, I want to delve in more deeply here to expose the strategies behind the approach that has worked for so many. Here we go

A Focus on Building the Habit

At the heart of Hello Mornings is one simple habit. We believe that if we can help you build the habit of meeting with Jesus—trusting that He has a plan for your life and living as though you trust that plan—that habit will grow, as habits always do. We also offer Bible studies, planning and fitness resources, and group challenges designed to help you build on that one foundational habit. Our focus isn't necessarily teaching in-depth Bible study methods, perfect planning techniques, or ideal fitness regimens. Yes, we introduce people to all of those, but our core purpose is to help you solidify the habits needed for each.

In just a few minutes each morning, anyone can attend to important yet often overlooked aspects of life—a relationship with God, planning the day, and improving health. The goal isn't overnight transformation but slow and steady progress toward lifelong habits that radically change the direction of our lives and allow us to thrive in whatever role God has given us.

We believe there is great power in small deeds done with great faithfulness.

The Three Essentials of the Habit

From the very first day of school, we learn a little bit of reading, a little bit of writing, and a little bit of arithmetic. We don't perfect our skills in one area and only then move on to the next. Our teachers don't lock up the reading books until we've learned our arithmetic or our writing. Each skill plays an important role. Simply buying gum at the store requires read ng, writing, and arithmetic. From a young age, we need basic abi ity in multiple areas to get through our day.

The same is true in our grown-up daily lives.

That's why in Hello Mornings we tie three essential areas into one habit: *God, Plan, Move.*

Each element is important to a well-lived life. Of course, our t me with God is by far the most important, but the ability to plan and manage our energy is also integral to walking out our faith and living life well.

God time, *Plan* time, and *Move* time all work *together* to he p us walk out our faith. To develop perfect, in-depth morn ng routines in all these areas could take a lifetime of work. But we can't wait a lifetime to connect with God, to live purposeful y, or to take care of the health God has given us.

Just as with reading, writing, and arithmetic, the power is in starting now and starting small. While one minute of prayer, planning, or exercise each day might seem silly, the impact of being a person who "exercises each day" or "plans every day" or "prays every day" cannot be overstated.

Even if it is for a tiny amount of time, the more we consistent y repeat a routine, the more we identify ourselves as action-oriented people who are constantly growing. Imagine after just one month being able to say, "I started every single day with Jesus for this whole month, *and* I was purposeful with my time, *and* I exercised every day. For a whole month." These may be small habits, but there is power in laying a solid foundation—and in knowing that you *can* be that person. It will bleed into the rest of your life in unexpected ways.

When I first met my husband, Jimmy, in college, it affected how I organized my day. If I knew he was going to be at the library at a certain time, lo and behold, I needed to be at the library at that very same time. Crazy coincidence . . . I not only changed my daily plans, but I also went to the gym a bit more and had fewer late-night cookie binges. My affection for him wasn't limited to the time I spent with him; it influenced the rest of my day and my choices as well.

We often hear about people making radical transformations in their health after having children. Some quit smoking. Some lose weight and build muscle. Some people change jobs or remove themselves from destructive friendships. When I became a mother, it affected every single area of my life—what I ate, what I read, what I watched on TV, and how I spent my time.

Our love for God should have every bit as much of an impact on our day-to-day lives.

The heart behind *God, Plan, Move* is to create an on-ramp for our *God* time to infiltrate the rest of our day. It starts with time in the Word and prayer, moving into prayerfully planning our day, and then ensuring we have the energy that day for whatever God may ask of us.

As you'll see in chapters 7 and 8, we ultimately pursue planning and fitness not because we want to be organized and fit. We do it because we want the Spirit of God, the truth of God, and the life of God in the very corners of our lives.

How *God*, *Plan*, and *Move* Work Together

To do anything well, we must first know our purpose, then create a plan to carry out that purpose, and finally have the energy to power that purpose. We can see the benefits of having a purpose, planning well, and having the power to follow through in almost every sphere of life. From the athletic arena to construction sites to the boardroom, these three elements are central.

A basketball player first meets with the coach, reviews the game plan, and then warms up before setting foot in the game. A musician connects with her band, reviews the set list, and tunes her instrument before stepping on stage. A businesswoman connects with her boss or her team, reviews the plan for the day, and then grabs some coffee before she tackles her to-do list.

These three elements of purpose, planning, and power correspond to the three parts of the *God, Plan, Move* concept.

We as believers, as ambassadors of Christ, should enter our days with every bit as much intention as an athlete steps onto the field or an entrepreneur enters a meeting—with faith-filled purpose, a plan, and the power to live it out.

While each element is very different, if we choose to tie them together, they can then be far more powerful than they ever were apart.

Think of it like a motorcycle. A motorcycle is made up of three primary elements that make it move: the engine, the frame, and the tires. All those components work together to create a final product that is efficient and effective. Separately, they range from less powerful to completely useless.

Our *God* time is like the engine that moves us, our *Plan* time is like the frame and handlebars that steer us where God leads, and our *Move* time is like the tires that allow us to progress easily.

We don't want to build an out-of-balance morning—all engine and no tires. We want our morning routine to be well-rounded and effective so that we can make the most of the days God has given to us.

Having our *God* time is essential. It is far and away the most important. But our *Plan* time and *Move* time put feet to our faith.

The Pharisees and Sadducees were experts on the Law, but they didn't allow it to influence how they lived. In Matthew 23, Jesus shared example after example of how they essentially missed the forest for the trees. They prided themselves on following the details of the Law but missed the heart of it. They knew it inside and out but failed in the application.

James calls us to be not only hearers of the Word but doers as well (James 1:22). If we are spending time with God, laying down our lives at His feet, doesn't it make sense to then lay our daily plans at His feet? Shouldn't our faith infiltrate how we live our lives and spend our time? If God has plans for our lives, shouldn't we make choices that help us have the energy to live out His great purpose for us today?

James 2:17–18 says, "Faith by itself, if it is not accompanied by action, is dead. But someone will say, 'You have faith; I have deeds.' Show me your faith without deeds, and I will show me my faith by my deeds."

I want to accompany my faith with action. I want to open my Bible with the mind-set that God may ask me to actively respond to what I hear from Him that day. So when I read about loving my neighbor, the rest of my morning routine offers a track to walk that out. I can add "make soup" to my daily plan, and then I can make sure that when I go on my daily walk, I bring the soup to drop by my ill neighbor's home.

We aren't only building isolated habits in our morning routines; we are also conditioning ourselves to be open and ready to respond to whatever God may lead us to do each day. That's why I don't want my lack of energy to cause me to walk right by the woman desperate for eye contact and a hug. I don't want my lack of planning to create a spiral of hurry and frustration. Instead, I want to have the wisdom, forethought, and energy to make choices that spread hope. Maybe my extra tenderness to my children will give them the security to ask the new child in class to join them for lunch. Maybe that friend connection will comfort that child's broken heart in the midst of her parents' divorce.

Never underestimate the impact of your life and the effect of living it well.

The Enemy wants you to believe you are small and that your life doesn't matter, when, in fact, God wants to use you to radically influence the world around you. If you're going to embrace God's plan, it will take some change—and change requires purpose, planning, and power.

God, Plan, Move.

A Simple Start for Your Morning Habit

The three-minute morning is a . . . three-minute morning routine (shocker, I know) that includes all three aspects of the

Hello Mornings *God, Plan, Move* concept. Starting small, it's a foundational routine that you can scale up as God leads.

Remember, everyone has three minutes every morning of their lives. So this routine eliminates the feeling of *I've got no time*—a common obstacle for not spending time with God, planning, or making healthy choices.

In a Hello Mornings survey, hundreds of women, more than 60 percent, said they need at least sixty minutes for a good *God, Plan, Move* morning routine. Nearly a third of those said ninety minutes were necessary. Well, no wonder we struggle! I don't know about you, but finding an extra hour or hour and a half in my morning is a Herculean feat. For most people, I'm not sure it's even possible without incredibly drastic measures.

The truth is, you can have a powerful morning routine in just three minutes. Suspend your disbelief for just a bit and hear me out. I know three minutes sounds small. But can I challenge you right now to do a solid minute of squats or push-ups? Not such a short amount of time, is it?

It's easy to waste time—hello, Internet—but it's also easy to extend it. Three truly focused minutes *can* have a real impact on your day. And if you then have that three-minute morning every single day? Wow—what a powerful foundation on which to build.

By building a consistent habit, we begin the process of labeling ourselves as women who nurture our relationship with God, live purposefully, and take care of our health.

Once we have the foundation, we can then scale up each area as God leads us to grow. The beauty is that when life hits us hard and we get sick or travel or even just wake up late, we can simply scale our routine back down to the three-minute morning habit we've built and never feel as though we've missed a day or failed at our morning routine. While it's a simple habit, when we've been consistent for a week or two, it feels like such an accomplishment. And it will reset our perspective on what we're capable of.

And remember, the goal isn't to stay at three minutes. Build the habit for thirty days. If at some point you want to scale up, go for it. But if it starts getting hard and you feel like quitting, scale it back down so keeping the habit is more central than having an impressive non-habit.

As I mentioned in chapter 1, the routine is fairly simple:

- *God* time: Pray Psalm 143:8
- *Plan* time: Review calendar
- *Move* time: Drink a glass of water

By the way, I recommend the exact same routine—same verse, same planning action, and same moving action every day for that first thirty days. Why? Because the simpler it is, the more likely you are to stick to it and build the habit. Of course, it's your habit to build, but I want to give you a good, solid starting place.

Anne Blackmore Keo shared her experience with the three-minute morning:

> At first I wasn't sure how much I would get out of the same verse every day for a month. But just in a few days I've seen the impact this one verse can have in such different ways. "Show me the way I should go, for to you I entrust my

life" allows me to pray through the mundane tasks of my day—my daily approach to parenting, teaching, and being a wife. And today I prayed this verse with a friend making scary big decisions for her teenage daughter. I know there is power in a Scripture verse; I just didn't expect this level of power in three minutes!

What If I Want More Than Three Minutes?

But maybe you want more than three minutes. If so, keep reading: I'm about to share a few ways to scale up each area of your morning routine. Just remember to keep the whole habit central. Don't go all crazy with one area and neglect the others. We can walk in incredible freedom when we're not weighted down by guilt for ignoring key areas of our lives.

Consistency counts. And all three concepts together—each as strong as the other—can take us further than any one can alone. So even as you build your habit, continue your three-minute morning.

Long-Term Change Versus Short-Term Change

Short-term change and long-term change require polar-opposite actions. Just as marathon runners' bodies look drastically different from those of sprinters, so our plans for our lives should look different when we are pursuing change at different levels.

Rarely do people embark on a new Bible study, planning, or fitness routine and truly think about the long term. Normally we think about the short-term results we want to see. *Reading through the Bible. Setting goals. Losing weight.* What if we changed our perspective and planned for the long term? What if we thought, *What can I do today to make this a habit I'll have when I'm ninety? How can I make myself not want to quit?*

This is why Hello Mornings is all about long-term change—so you won't *want* to quit, and you *will* be more likely to have this habit when you're ninety.

What does long-term change look like? It's taking small bites It's giving yourself grace. It's focusing your energy on continuing rather than moving fast. It's the tortoise and not the hare. Long-term change doesn't look impressive. Endurance is rarely noticed until the end. We all love to be fast. We love to be cheered on. But the truth is that marathon runners run much of the race alone. They have to have motivation beyond the praise of others.

Sometimes in our pursuit of personal change, we get so much satisfaction from sharing our fast, impressive plans with those around us that we lose our desire for the reward of the end result. Even worse, we forget the satisfaction found in the journey.

A three-minute goal may not bring applause, but it will bring results. What we do daily will invariably grow. So those three *consistent* minutes will likely grow into ten, twenty, or thirty minutes every day. And even just a ten-minute morning routine adds up to sixty hours of intentional time over the course of a year.

It's so easy to think that to live a healthy life we need to make a massive leap. We need to make a big jump to cross that chasm. But, in reality, it's more like that scene in Indiana Jones when he comes to a deep gorge, and rather than leaping, he follows the clues laid out before him and simply takes one small step after another. Magically, as he steps, the real pathway appears over the gorge and, baby step by baby step, he makes it across.

Maybe the same is true for our lives. We see a massive gap between the women we want to be and the women we are today, and we think we need to transform like Cinderella. Overnight transformation is all the rage. We want to see the difference to feel the change. We want others to notice and be wowed.

But the only thing true about overnight transformation is that, just like with Cinderella, the easier the change, the easier it is to change back. The clock always strikes midnight.

Maybe the only way to cross the great gorge of change is not to focus on the other side but to focus on the step right in front of us. Maybe if we think of it less like a leap and more like a journey, we'll be more likely to take actions today that line up with who we want to be tomorrow.

We make thousands of decisions each day. What if we invested our energy into making each one a wise decision that lines up with our dreams, instead of focusing on what we aren't? If we focus on our daily decisions, instead of looking for a silver bullet, we'll eventually find ourselves where we want to be.

The truth is, this is a lifelong journey. The woman on the other side of the gorge of change is the result of thousands, maybe millions, of day-to-day decisions. Step by step. Morning by morning.

Decisions

If long-term change starts with our daily decisions, how do we make those thousands of good decisions each day?

We have to start well. Our first decisions need to be good ones. Better yet, the longer we can delay decision-making, the more likely we are to make more good decisions throughout the day. What do I mean?

Decision-making is exhausting. It requires willpower, which, as research has shown, is a limited resource. In 1998, Roy Baumeister and colleagues did a study, commonly known as the "Chocolate and Radish Study," in which they invited participants into a room where chocolate-chip cookies had just been baked. Researchers assigned the participants to eat from either the plate of cookies or from a bowl of radishes. After eating from their assigned dish, participants were then given a puzzle that, unbeknownst to them, was unsolvable. Those who were assigned to eat from the radish bowl and had to exercise willpower to avoid the cookies consequently gave up on the puzzle twice as fast as the cookie group and the control group (which had no snack).[1] The finding from this study, and subsequent related ones, was that our willpower is like a muscle, and it can be depleted.

So if we can start our days with a series of good habits, we can save all that willpower for other choices later in the day when we are tired. You see, habits don't require thought. I'll explain more about habits in detail later on, but the key is to understand that as we develop a habit, we build neural pathways in our brains and strengthen them with every repetition of that action until it's almost second nature. Habits, once established, require minimal energy. They put our brains and willpower on autopilot. So the more good things we can turn into habits, the more we can save our decision-making for other parts of our lives. And as we grow our habits (and build good ones), we gradually develop into the people we long to be.

Our character is the sum of our habits—which is why Hello Mornings encourages a morning habit.

Let's make starting our day at the throne of God our default. Let's make living intentionally our habit. Let's make healthy choices our norm. Let's make small, simple steps an essential element in living an exceptional life.

Author Anthony Trollope wrote, "A small daily task, if it be really daily, will beat the labors of a spasmodic Hercules."[2]

If that isn't the best phrase ever, I don't know what is. I can certainly relate to being a spasmodic Hercules. It tends to hit me around January 1, when the New Year's resolution discussion is at its fever pitch. I get carried away and make plans that I could never manage in the long term. My spasmodic Hercules resolutions leave me on February's curb like an after-midnight Cinderella.

How can we take what we've learned about ourselves and the core Hello Mornings concepts and put them into practice? We simply have to incorporate the three essential activities of *God* time, *Plan* time, and *Move* time into our daily routine.

The Three Steps of Change

I was six years old, in my grandfather's pontoon boat with my dad and brother, cruising around Green Lake, a decidedly not-green, beautiful, clear lake in Wisconsin that's bordered by trees and cliffs. My overly imaginative little brain was bursting with all of the possibilities of our adventure that day. I might catch a bajillion fish to bring back to the lake house for my grandma to fry with her special recipe. Or maybe we'd discover a new inlet that was a secret cove for pirates and I'd solve a police-baffling mystery just like Nancy Drew. Or maybe Daddy would let me drive the boat, and I'd navigate the lake with the expertise of a seasoned captain, and then he'd let me drive the car home to Chicago on Sunday.

As I sat with my brother in the front of the boat, imagining all that the day might hold, we were oblivious to a storm rolling in. But when my normally calm father began barking orders, we knew something was wrong. That something was that the engine had just died and he couldn't get it started. To make matters worse, a lot worse, our now engineless boat was being quickly swept toward the cliffs by the winds of the incoming storm.

I'd like to say I handled the situation with a cool, calm, and collected attitude. But then I'd be lying and describing my brother and dad, not me. I was freaking out. From my perspective, we were doomed. There was a raging storm, we had no motor, and that cliff loomed large. I was overwhelmed by my visions of our boat crashing into a thousand pieces against the jagged rocks of the cliff. I pictured my six-year-old self struggling to swim all the way past the massive rocks to the beach. My eyes were glued on the clouds rolling in.

My father could have adopted the same perspective. Thankfully, he didn't. Instead of focusing on what we didn't have, he evaluated what we did have.

He saw that although we didn't have a motor, we did have an anchor. And with his solution-oriented perspective, he realized that the anchor was our key to getting out of there.

He threw it far overboard on the furthest side away from the cliffs and cranked the boat to the anchor. Over and over he threw that anchor out and pulled our boat to it and away from the cliffs as the storm raged on.

Finally, soaking wet and exhausted, we made it back to the safety of our pier.

Wouldn't it be great if we could wake up with purpose each morning and not encounter any storms in life? Wouldn't it be lovely if we could dream and do without any waves to knock us down?

The reality is, storms, both big and small, are a part of our everyday lives. And from our perspective, it might seem impossible to have a consistent, purposeful morning routine. It seems too hard to build a habit.

Two things saved us that day on Green Lake: my father's perspective and the power of our anchor. Instead of focusing on the cliffs and the storm and what could happen, he looked around at what we did have that could change our situation. Because of his perspective, he was able to recognize how the anchor could rescue us. Not only did it keep us from crashing into the cliffs, but by using the anchor in a creative way, my dad moved us to safety.

We don't usually think of anchors as powerful. Boat owners don't sit around the marina bragging about them. They talk about the speed of their vessels and horsepower of their engines. They probably talk about everything except their anchors.

But while a boat is powerless without a motor, it will be

only a fleeting memory without an anchor. An anchor keeps it from floating away with the waves. A well-used anchor can even save a father and his children from a very dangerous situation.

Just as my gloom-and-doom perspective on that boat kept me from doing anything remotely helpful, wrong perspectives about our mornings, our abilities, or our situations will predispose us to failure.

And then just as our anchor kept us steady in the storm, if we build a simple anchor in our mornings, like the three-minute morning routine, we can keep our habits afloat no matter how the waves crash down.

Finally, just as my dad chose to keep moving rather than staying where he first dropped the anchor, we, too, can keep moving and developing our morning routine so we are ever growing in our relationship with God and His calling in our lives.

It's Time to Get Started

We've covered a lot so far. We've talked about why your mornings matter and how you can learn how you're wired so you can make a tailored morning routine. We've learned about the heart and idea behind *God, Plan, Move* and creating a morning routine for the long term.

Now we're ready to dive in to building your very own morning routine. The rest of this book is going to follow the steps I alluded to in my boat story. For each area of our morning routine, *God* time, *Plan* time, and *Move* time, we'll show you a three-step process to starting and building your morning routine.

You will:

1. shift your perspective on each area of your morning routine,
2. set your anchor habit for each area of your morning routine, and
3. start growing in each area of your morning routine.

The next few chapters on *God, Plan, Move* share a perspective-altering insight, a simple anchor to get you started, and then a variety of ideas to keep you growing.

This isn't about overnight transformation or rigid formulas. I want to help you start small, be faithful, and grow consistently. It's against the grain of our culture to be okay with small, but small seems to be a part of God's upside-down kingdom. He has a history of taking weaknesses and feeble steps of faith and magnifying them for His glory and for the good of others. He *doesn't* have a history of taking massive, accomplished deeds and hijacking them for His glory.

He didn't wait for Moses to be a confident speaker (Ex. 4). He didn't wait for David to be the biggest and strongest (1 Sam. 16). He didn't wait for Rahab to have a perfect reputation (Josh. 2). He didn't wait for Mary to have a husband (Matt. 1). He didn't wait for Saul to come to his own logical conclusion (Acts 9).

He doesn't need our achievements; He wants our attention.

Let's get started.

part two

Your Morning
Routine Blueprint

five

God Time

My four-year-old son, Jackson, was trying to get his straw in the juice pouch when he got lost in the food court crowd. I thought he was right behind me, but when we finally found a table and turned around, we saw he wasn't there. I figured he couldn't have gone far. In fact, he was probably near the live performance happening over by the stage. I looked everywhere for his red-and-brown striped shirt and khaki cargo shorts, but I didn't see him.

As fear started to rise in my throat, I called his name. Surely he was around the food court somewhere. A few minutes went by, and I still couldn't find him. I walked around, frantically yelling his name louder and louder.

One by one, people came up to me. "Is someone you love lost? How can I help? What is his name? What is he wearing? How old is he?"

Complete strangers were willing to act like fools running around yelling the name of a boy they'd never even met.

Five minutes went by. Ten minutes went by. Fifteen minutes went by.

I felt as though my heart stopped beating. Had someone taken him? How could he have gotten so far away? Was there an accident of some kind? So many fears swirled in my head.

In the meantime another mom, busy with her own kids and with plenty on her mind, saw a little boy sitting alone on a bench. He looked scared and alone and was fumbling with the button on his pocket. She put everything she was doing on hold and walked over to him.

"Can I help you?"

She knew what it meant for a mama to lose her baby. She helped him open his shorts pocket, and she called the number on the paper. A few minutes later, I was the happiest, most thankful mom in the world.

Shift Your *God*-Time Perspective

One of the most important reasons we start every day with Jesus is not that it's something to check off our Christian to-do list. It's important because God loves His children unfathomably, even more than I love my son, and He's asking you and me to help reach them. He doesn't need us to preach from the rooftops. He just wants us to be willing to come before Him each day and ask, "Is someone you love lost? How can I help?"

Shift 1: It's Not About a Checklist

Maybe God wants you to reach out to a neighbor today. Maybe someone in your home or a stranger at the store needs an encouraging word or a smile. Maybe you'll simply inspire others by the choices you make and the way you live the day. You may never know. But if you take the time to ask Him each morning, you just might get to be the rescuer who leads someone back to their Father who loves them more than life itself.

Maybe the person God wants to rescue is you. To have you come close each day to hear how He loves you and cares for you. To give you time to lay your burdens at His feet. Maybe you have deep hurts that need to be healed before you can even think about helping others, and daily time with God is the remedy.

Whatever the reason, the fact is that the most powerful thing we can do is build a habit of listening to God each day. To bring Him glory, to remember His goodness, and to steady our hearts before the storms hit, begin the day by studying His Word, praying, and worshipping.

No program, self-help book, course, or video could help you more. No mentor, pastor, or counselor can more effectively heal your hurts than meeting with God each day. Those are all wonderful and needed things, but He must be our foundation. He knows us, understands us, and loves us more than we can comprehend.

He is simply worthy of our time, our energy, and our efforts. We were made to worship Him, and when we have rightly tuned our hearts to His, we can be a part of the symphony He is conducting.

If God created us, loves us, and gives us purpose, why would we face a single day apart from Him? It makes so much sense when I think about it, but in my real, day-to-day life, it can be a challenge.

Why is it so hard to have consistent time with God?

Let's play the word association game. I say "quiet time," you say . . .

Guilt.

Something I used to do.

Something I don't do enough.

Something I don't know how to do.

We know we *should* have a quiet time every day, but that somehow leads to feelings of guilt when we don't achieve it. The problem is that when we feel guilty, we tend to avoid. Have you ever noticed that? If you don't have time for your normal *God* time, you move it to later in the day or skip it altogether. Then, the next morning, you feel so guilty about it that you skip it again.

But there's something more to focus on—a deeper issue with the way we view our daily relationship with God. I pray it will heap grace upon you and free you from that guilt.

Shift 2: Focus on Persistence, Not Perfection

We often think of our quiet time as one big chunk of an event. That our quiet time has to be our Bible study, worship, prayer, and everything related to God all wrapped up in one solid hour and neatly packaged in the early morning.

But as life moves through its seasons, the perfect quiet-time trifecta becomes more difficult to find. So we wait because we've fallen for the lie that it doesn't count if we only read one verse. It has to be thirty minutes or an hour. We have to get through the whole study passage for the day. We must fill out all the pages or pray all the prayers.

But we don't really have to do all the things; we just need to do one thing. We just need to start somewhere. Once we start, we can learn to adjust to whatever time we have and grow from there.

Have you ever been to a symphony? World-class musicians take the stage and get settled. Then after a short pause, the concertmaster—the first violinist—comes out to applause. She bows and then does something that seems odd. She turns to the orchestra, all eyes on her, and she plays one note. One single note. Then the rest of the musicians tune their instruments. It sounds like cacophony. But soon enough, they're done, and all is quiet. After another pause, the conductor comes out to applause.

In some of my children's orchestras, I've then seen the conductor take one or two students' instruments and tune them. It can seem like an awkward time, but the conductor knows how crucial it is that every instrument is perfectly in tune. One off string can wreak havoc in the whole orchestra.

After everyone is in tune, and all eyes are on the conductor, they dive into the music, and the symphony begins.

I want you to think of your morning time with God like a symphony. There are two essential parts: the first is tuning your heart to Him through worship and prayer, and the second is Bible study. Just as the musicians start by making sure their instruments are in tune so the rest of the concert sounds good, it's important, no matter how busy we are, that we take the time to tune in to God's heart.

So many of us skip or miss our morning *God* time because we think we don't have time. But when we break it up into the two parts, we can recognize that we *always* have time to start our day with God, even when we don't have time for in-depth Bible study or journaling.

Set Your *God*-Time Anchor

Setting your anchor is all about beginning your day on the right foot and with the right mind-set. God has a purpose for you. For your life, your years, your months, your days . . . for today. Start your day with Him—even if just for a few moments—to connect with Him and find out what that purpose might be.

Have you ever seen football players drive up to the field, jump out of their cars, and run straight onto the field for the championship game? No, that would be ridiculous. That would never happen. They always connect with the coach first. They need to know the game plan and where they fit in.

For you, this can be simple daily prayer while you're lying in bed. Or it might be a muttered prayer while you hit the snooze button or race through the house. It might be a recited memory verse and worship time as you drive through town. It might be a Bible verse on a sticky note and a heartfelt time of listening as you brush your teeth.

I pray Psalm 143:8 every morning. Maybe another verse speaks to your heart, or maybe you do something different to connect with God each morning. The key, though, is to take that first moment to connect. To tune your heart to His. We may not have time to dive into Scripture deeply every day, but we do always, always have time to be intentional and surrender our day to Him. To say, "Let the morning bring me word of your unfailing love, for I have put my trust in you. Show me the way I should go, for to you I entrust my life" (Ps. 143:8).

Then, as you have time, study the Bible, pray, worship, journal, do your thing.

Just as we start each day by saying good morning to our

loved ones, we can say good morning to God, listen, and worship with intention, even if it's only a moment. We don't ignore our family if we can't sit down for thirty minutes or an hour. If I'm running late, I don't tell my husband, "I'm sorry, I can't acknowledge you right now because I only have five minutes." No, we do whatever we can to connect with them, whether it's squeezing in a quick hug before we fly out the door or sitting down to breakfast and conversation.

We adjust our time to our circumstances, but we don't skip it and wait until all the stars align and we have the perfect amount of time, the right morning light, and plenty of peace and quiet.

We do ourselves and our relationship with God a great service when we choose to connect in any way we can, even on our busy days. It is always time well spent.

This is the start. This is setting your anchor with the first essential activity of *God* time. You can start every single day with Him—no matter how busy, sick, or tired you are.

In the three-minute morning, we encourage women to read and memorize Psalm 143:8, but that's really just a guide. You can tweak the three-minute morning however you like. Here are some ideas:

- Set your phone alarm to show a verse or prayer point.
- Listen to a worship song.
- Tell God what you're thankful for.
- Thank God for who He is and how wonderful He is.
- Remember God's good deeds.
- Pray using one or more scripture.
- Keep a prayer calendar on your bathroom mirror.

If you don't use Psalm 143:8, what will your *God*-time anchor be?

_____

_____

_____

_____

Start Growing Your *God* Time

As important as it is to set your anchor, you also need to grow in your knowledge of God's Word and prayer.

One of my favorite morning habits is to write out part of a book of the Bible in a simple spiral-bound notebook. It may sound impressive, but some mornings it's just one verse. Other mornings it's twenty. But I know that my mornings start with my Bible, my spiral notebook, and my favorite pen. There's something incredibly cathartic about slowly writing out the Word of God.

I have terrible handwriting, so I write very intentionally, concentrating on each word. The physical motion wakes me up and gets my brain and body in sync, and the slowness of writing, versus simply reading, forces me to think about the passage and its meaning.

Rather than rushing through a reading of a passage or trying to finish a certain Bible study section, I start my morning slowly and intentionally, and I build each day until I've filled the worn, coffee-stained notebooks on my shelf with handwritten books of the Bible. I love the gift I've created to someday pass on to my children.

What could your first step be? Maybe it's just slowly reading through the Bible. Use an old-fashioned bookmark, and start from the beginning. Don't worry about how many chapters you read or don't read each day. Just start your day reading the Word.

Maybe for you, it's listening through the Bible using an audiobook. Maybe it's daily scripture memory—marinating in one passage at a time. There are so many ways to study the Bible. From character studies to book studies to word studies—your options are endless.

Whatever it is, I encourage you to find a simple study method to start your day. If you need some ideas, you can check out the Hello Mornings Big Bible Study Idea List in the appendix where I've listed a few of my favorite study methods.

Other powerful components of your quiet time might include the following:

- Prayer

  I have specific things I pray for each day. You can download my prayer calendars at HelloMornings.org to see, for example, the topics I pray for my husband and my children. I also keep a list in my to-do app for all the prayer requests that pop up during the day.
- Journaling

  Journaling is another popular option. There is something truly powerful about slowing down and writing. You can write out prayers, memories, gratitude lists, and Bible verses as you journal during your *God* time.
- Worship

  And, finally, there are so many ways to experience worship. Ideas include listening to worship songs, reading

Scripture aloud about who and how great God is, writing out a list of praise or thanks, playing an instrument and singing, or rewriting a psalm in your own words.

New York Times bestselling author Melanie Shankle offered me this simple tip: "I am a big fan of writing Bible verses on notecards and taping them to my bathroom mirror. It's an easy way to make sure that I start my day focused on what matters most."

Chrystal Evans Hurst shared this encouragement:

Before you get going in the morning, surrender your day to God. Stretch your hands to heaven before your feet hit the floor, and tell Him that you want to do what's important to Him in your day. Don't let the urgent dictate the important. Allow God to guide and direct your steps . . . before you step out of the bed.

Cathy Payne Minson said:

God time for me is after my three-minute morning is complete. I go to my favorite comfy and cozy spot and curl up. My Bible, journal, and book are waiting for me. I set a cup of hot tea next to me on the table. I pray, letting the Lord know if I am ready to see something in Scripture or hear something in prayer. I read Scripture, journal, then pray. I read up to a chapter in whichever book I am studying, make notes, then pray. I pray about my day ahead, challenges from the day before, requests for myself and others, praises, and then I listen. Depending on the appointment schedule for the day, this final prayer might be done in the shower. Sometimes I think I listen more when I pray in the shower. Probably because I know there will be no interruptions.

The Impact of God Time

My grandmother-in-law is from Verdun, France. She lived through the Nazi occupation as a small child and often tells us stories after Easter dinner. I'm always in awe of the hardships so many endured and the courage they revealed in the process.

Researcher Philip Hallie wrote about a small village in France called Le Chambon. During World War II and the Nazi occupation of France, the people in that simple village rescued more than three thousand Jews. They were not relatives, friends, or associates. They were simply people who needed saving. What fascinates me is that as Hallie researched, he imagined Le Chambon to be a town of brave, daring, and courageous people. What he discovered upon visiting the town and interviewing the people was that there was nothing particularly outstanding about any of them.

The only fact that united them was that Sunday after Sunday, they went to church and listened to the sermons of their pastor, André Trocmé. Month after month and year after year, they learned about what it meant to follow God and do the right thing. Out of faith and habit, they became an entire town of people who, when faced with evil, knew what to do and simply did it.

One villager is quoted by American theologian and United Methodist Church bishop Dr. William H. Willimon as saying,

"Pastor always taught us that there comes a time in every life when a person is asked to do something for Jesus. When our time came, we knew what to do."[1]

When my time comes, will I know what to do? When your time comes, will you know what to do? Will either of us even recognize our call to courage? It might be a daring rescue operation or simply helping a lost and lonely four-year-old boy.

Our daily time with God is more than just plowing through a Bible study. It's about learning more of His Word, bringing that knowledge and power with us into the rest of the day, and praying for a heart in tune with His to respond to the needs all around us.

six

Plan Time

We had a six-month-old, a two-year-old, and bags under our eyes as big as Mary Poppins's suitcase. That particular Sunday, despite our weariness, we got them dressed and to church—mostly on time. Once they got settled in the makeshift nursery, we set out to find the sanctuary.

Don't worry; we weren't so exhausted that we couldn't find our own church sanctuary. That Sunday was part of our church's yearly missions conference. Thousands of people from all across the world gathered, and we needed a bigger location, so the church service was held at our local convention center.

Frankly, Jimmy and I hadn't gotten out much since becoming parents. We had a steady routine of feedings, diapers, the occasional bit of sleep, and church. As I sat there in an unfamiliar building, worshipping with so many new people, I felt energized by my new surroundings. I looked around at all the people who had traveled far and wide to join us. I wondered where they'd come from and what their journeys were like.

In an uncharacteristic bout of spontaneity, I leaned over to Jimmy and whispered, "We need to go on vacation."

He looked at me with a puzzled expression that morphed into acceptance and then excitement. "Okay," he said.

I leaned over again and whispered, "Today."

Once the shock wore off, I could see the gears in his brain working things out. *Do I have the vacation time? Is it in the budget? Where to go? What to pack?* We both got silly smiles on our faces, and right there in the middle of church, we decided we'd skip our traditional after-church meal and go on vacation instead.

We drove home like kids headed to a candy store. As soon as the girls were settled for their afternoon naps, we packed the car; and the minute they woke up we headed off with our only decision. North. (When you live in Central Texas, there aren't many other options.)

It was such a thrill to be on the road with no particular plans. Me, the mom who kept detailed records of feedings, diaper changes, and doctor's appointments. Jimmy, our super trip planner extraordinaire. We felt fun and carefree. It seemed less about the destination and more about enjoying the journey.

We originally decided to go to Nashville, but after six hours in the car with a baby and a toddler, we decided Hot Springs, Arkansas, was the perfect location for our first family vacation. We had a wonderful time hiking and visiting historical spots and candy shops. We've been back as a family many times—most of those were also spontaneous trips (or at least spontaneous as far as the kids knew).

But that first spontaneous Hot Springs family vacation was *very* different from a trip Jimmy and I had taken three years earlier. We had just worked ridiculously hard to pay off our college loans. (Oh, the stories I could tell.) As a reward to ourselves, we decided to take a trip to Europe.

I realize that might sound incredibly extravagant for a couple that not two years before was tens of thousands of dollars in college debt. But Jimmy had a lot of family in Europe: his dad was stationed in France, his aunt was a US Army officer stationed in Germany, and he had extended family throughout France. We needed only to pay for our plane tickets (which were very cheap at the time) and take a little spending money. To maximize our budget, we planned every detail of the trip. We had an itinerary and researched every plane ticket and train ticket, and we were even able to squeeze in a short stay in Paris at a bed-and-breakfast before our return flight home. Our planning squeezed incredible memories out of that journey on a newlywed budget.

It was a wonderful trip. We met so many of Jimmy's French family members, saw and read about fascinating historical locations, and enjoyed every minute of the thoroughly thought-out, extremely planned trip.

There are seasons to plan and seasons to be spontaneous, but a good plan can take us places we never dreamed we could go.

Shift Your *Plan*-Time Perspective

As Christians, many of us struggle with planning because we see it as something separate from God. How can we plan our day if we are putting our faith in Him? How can we set goals and have schedules if we are following where God leads us?

Shift 1: Planning Is Something We Do with God

Scripture tells two kinds of stories: There was Noah, who followed a plan down to the cubic inch, and then Ruth, who made a spontaneous decision. There was Nehemiah, who planned the rebuilding of the wall, and Peter, who jumped out of the boat in the middle of a storm.

Even Scripture makes planning and faith seem like opposites. For instance, Matthew 6:34 says, "Therefore do not worry about tomorrow, for tomorrow will worry about itself. Each day has enough trouble of its own." But Proverbs 21:5 says, "The plans of the diligent lead to profit as surely as haste leads to poverty."

So is planning good or . . . bad?

Part of the beauty of our trip to Hot Springs was the sheer freedom of it. In the midst of a very demanding season of parenting, it was refreshing to wing it. At the same time, part of the beauty of our trip to Europe was savoring every detail and planning it together.

There are seasons to plan and seasons to be flexible. Our lack of planning wasn't more holy than our detailed planning. To always rely on a plan is not healthy. To always blow with the wind is not healthy. Doing a little of both, as God leads, will get you where you need to go.

Shift 2: Planning Connects the Dots

It becomes even clearer if we tweak the words *faith* and *planning* just a little. Another way to look at faith is trust, and another way to look at planning is stewardship. We trust in God and lean on Him for our every step, but we also choose to steward well the time, resources, and direction He gives us.

Really, faith and planning aren't on opposite ends of the spectrum; they are on opposite sides of the same coin.

Planning isn't something we do apart from God; it's something we do with Him. It is the bridge between the listening and obeying, between the calling and sending, between hearing and doing. Planning connects the dots of our faith.

Faith provides the vision and purpose for our planning. God often gives us direction, but He doesn't give us an itemized, step-by-step checklist. Without faith, planning makes no sense. But faith combined with planning brings clarity and direction. Like the lines in a dot-to-dot puzzle.

A woman might feel called to be a missionary. That is a dot of faith. The country she feels called to minister in is another dot of faith, but she has the freedom and, in fact, responsibility to draw the logistical lines of packing and raising support and eventually moving. She relies on God to reveal the dots and give her direction, but then God allows her to steward the plan.

Changing careers may be a step of faith, but organizing a résumé and scheduling interviews are how our plans can connect the dots of our faith.

Deciding how to educate our children is a dot of faith, but filling out paperwork or ordering resources are the plans we need to make to take our steps to the next dot.

Our faith is central, but our prayer-based plans are important and needed.

Do you see how planning and faith are tied together?

Planning goes awry when we go it alone and lose sight of the greater purpose. Planning isn't bad for my marriage unless I make plans without my husband. Planning isn't bad for my job unless I make plans without my boss. Planning isn't bad for my faith unless I make plans without God.

Our plans should begin and end with God. We plan with Him in the beginning and lay our plans at His feet along the way. In fact, I believe planning is a natural extension of our worship. If we believe God made us for a purpose and has a plan for our lives, then isn't the next logical step to order our lives around His plans, as far as we can see them?

David made plans to build a temple for God (1 Chron. 28). Nehemiah planned the rebuilding of the wall in Jerusalem (Neh. 3). Noah followed a plan for building the ark (Gen. 6). Planning isn't deciding where to go; it's deciding how to get where God leads. Our schedules and our plans should always be a sacrifice rather than an idol. It's all too easy to take control and cling tightly to our plans, but "unless the LORD builds the house, the builders labor in vain" (Ps. 127:1). As we connect the dots of our faith, we must hold our plans with open hands, intentionally keeping our trust in God rather than ourselves.

Shift 3: Don't Sweat the Small Stuff

Please note that when I talk about praying over our plans, it's not so much about fretting over whether God wants us to do the laundry today or tomorrow, but rather asking, *Are the things filling my day the things You want to fill my day? Am I running around trying to make myself feel important and productive, like Martha, when maybe what's truly needed is for me to sit awhile, like Mary [Luke 10:38–42]? Am I so focused on my own goals, like the priest in the story of the good Samaritan, that I walk right by those beaten and bruised all around me [Luke 10:25–37]?*

There is a very distinct difference between praying over every minor detail of our days because we don't know what God wants and submitting every moment of our days to His leading.

When I'm getting ready to make dinner, I don't tell my husband what I'm making and ask if he'll like it. We've been married nineteen years. I already know that he doesn't want anything with teriyaki sauce, Brussels sprouts, or exotic seafood. I know that anything with a large portion of meat is a win. And I know that a baguette earns extra wifey points.

On the other hand, when I invite guests over, I ask about allergies and food preferences. I suggest meals and ask if they will work for them. I may not know what they like or dislike because I may not know them very well yet. If I asked my husband about every single item I put on the dinner table, it would be clear to everyone that I didn't know Jimmy well.

Our planning should be an outpouring of the relationship we are fostering in our *God* time. As we build our relationship with the Lord, we better understand Him and His direction for our lives. The more we read His Word and listen for His still, small voice, the more available we'll be when He wants us to speak a word of hope or encouragement to someone.

So when it comes to planning, don't sweat the small stuff, but rather trust that as you pursue God, read His Word, and connect with Him through prayer, He'll lead you and guide you.

Our *Plan* time is simply aligning the rest of our day with God's heart

Set Your *Plan*-Time Anchor

Just like with our *God* time, we need to set our anchor each morning for *Plan* time. When we build a morning routine of connecting with God and then prayerfully plan our day, we lay a secure foundation for whatever lies ahead. We know whose we are, and we know where we are headed.

But it doesn't have to be complicated. My *Plan*-time anchor always follows my *God*-time anchor. As soon as I pray through Psalm 143:8, I take a quick look at my calendar for the day. It doesn't take any brainpower or critical thinking. I'm just checking in to see what I had already decided was important that day.

Do I have any appointments? Meetings? Is it anyone's birthday or anniversary? Or could it be someone's half birthday? In our family, we celebrate half birthdays. Nothing fancy. We just sing half of a birthday song and eat half of a birthday cake. Sometimes the kids will make a half card too. But since I don't have those dates memorized yet, if I don't check the calendar, I could miss them altogether.

Whether it's for a half birthday, a meeting, or an appointment, no one likes to feel unprepared. Checking my calendar every morning gives me a grid not only for what is going to happen that day but also how much room, if any, I have to add to it. I also use this opportunity to ask God if there is anyone I should pray for or reach out to that day.

What do you need help with when it comes to planning? Maybe you need to review your calendar, or maybe you've got that memorized and what you really need to do is simply write two or three items on a to-do list. The three-minute morning is a guide. You can swap out any action for something that will suit you better; but remember that the goal is to keep it super small so you can do it every day, rain or shine.

Here are some ideas for your *Plan*-time anchor:

- Review your calendar.
- Write down three to-do items.
- Read through your goals.
- Review an existing to-do list, if you have one.
- Arrange existing tasks for the day by priority.
- Pray over your calendar, asking God if anything needs to change.
- Pray over your to-do list, asking God if anything needs to change.
- Review your personal mission statement.
- Review any projects you have going.

What will your morning *Plan*-time anchor be? Remember to make it a ridiculously simple action that can get you going in the right direction every single day.

_____

_____

_____

_____

Hello Mornings participant Mariecris writes out a "dream list" during her *Plan* time. She starts by "just taking a few moments to make a dream to-do list for that day and circling the have-tos (usually two things for me) and then allowing grace for not completing the others. The next day, I create a new dream to-do list. It changes every day for me, and then just circle two again."

With small children and a busy family schedule, Mariecris benefits from the consistent yet flexible routine.

Others prefer more detail to help them navigate a full day. Melissa Q. said:

> Huge fan of three MITs [Most Important Tasks] here! And the other thing that has been crazy helpful for me is to have an idea of *when* I'm going to do those things. So, beside every task, I put a letter code (like *M* for morning or *AS* for after school or *E* for evening). This is especially helpful on crazy heavy to-do list days because I can just focus on the *M* tasks (for example) in the morning and disregard everything else, which helps me be not so overwhelmed with *all the things.*

Do you thrive with guided flexibility or clear details? Shape your three-minute morning and your *Plan*-time anchor to fit your personality and your season.

Start Growing Your *Plan* Time

The tricky part about planning is that it's so easy to get caught up in things that simply don't matter. We can learn how to be excellent at planning a million tasks, but if they aren't the right tasks, we are just spinning our wheels.

If we are clear on our priorities and consider them in the practical actions of everyday life, then the productivity method takes a back seat. The current obsession with productivity methods is a bit like being obsessed with the kind of Band-Aid we want to use rather than sweeping up the broken glass. We can have the perfect planner and task-capturing method, but if we aren't doing what matters, then none of it matters.

First things first. Knowing our priorities gets to the heart of planning. And priorities are inextricably linked to purpose, of which God is the only distributor. It's one thing to be efficient. Efficiency means getting a lot done in a small amount of time. It's quite another thing to be effective. Effectiveness means getting the right things done.

There are myriad books and tips on being efficient. I'd rather encourage you to focus on being effective. We do this by keeping God's big "dots" in mind so we can connect them. We prioritize His priorities. We remember why we are doing all the little day-to-day tasks. We make sure we aren't just adding things to our list arbitrarily. We add them because they will get us to our goal, God's dot for us.

Priorities, Processes, and Practical Actions

Effective planning involves three different phases. First, priorities make up the overarching vision we have for our time and our lives. The second phase is nailing down the processes or methods we use to manage our tasks. The third is enacting our processes on the practical level, through the small tasks we do each day.

The challenge is that we can easily spend all our time drowning in the practical tasks or building our processes while never examining or determining our priorities. The phrase "Can't see the forest for the trees" is right at home when it comes to planning. We get caught up in the day-to-day "urgent" matters that arise. As if we're caught in a riptide in the ocean, we slowly drift away from where we thought we were headed.

That's why I encourage you to grow your planning ability by focusing first on your priorities. Have you ever taken the time to verbalize your priorities? Do you know what they are? Do you know what order they are in? How well does your real-life schedule match up with your priorities?

I heard someone once describe priorities in terms of concentric circles, like an archery target. The most important things are in the center, and the others radiate outward: God, family, friends, calling (whether that's your job, ministry, or hobby), and so forth. Whenever anything isn't going well in an inner circle, we need to pull our energy back from the outer-circle areas until we've resolved the inner circle issues.

Phase 1: Determine Your Priorities

Several years ago, I took the time to create a personal mission statement. It didn't take long—just an hour or two at a coffee shop—but it's been instrumental in my ability to keep first things first in my life. When work feels full, I remember that work isn't at the top of my list; God and my family are. While work may fill some days, if things aren't right between God and me or between a family member and me, I need to scale back in some way and give attention to my true priorities.

I challenge you to schedule a coffee (or tea or soda) date with yourself and create your personal mission statement. It doesn't need to be fancy. It doesn't need to sound official. The point of writing a mission statement is simply to determine and verbalize our priorities. By writing them down and reminding ourselves day by day what is truly important, we won't be overwhelmed by the tyranny of the urgent.[1]

When our priorities are clear, we are more likely to align our time with our values. Too often, we fill our time with whatever comes our way, leaving us feeling out of control. It's easy to think that we don't have enough time, but if we're honest with ourselves, we have enough time for whatever is truly important. Time is simply our scapegoat. I like the perspective shift offered by Laura Vanderkam: "Instead of saying, 'I don't have time,' try saying 'it's not a priority,' and see how that feels. . . . Changing our language reminds us that time is a choice. If we don't like how we're spending an hour, we can choose differently."[2]

So instead of saying, "I don't have time to exercise or read my Bible," try saying, "Exercising and Bible reading aren't my priority." If that feels awful, perhaps it's time to do some realignment.

Brutal, isn't it? The truth hurts. Ever since I heard this quote, I haven't been able to get it out of my head. Especially as I've been working hard to finish this book, I've had to say no to several things. When I realize that saying no isn't a matter of time but priority, it makes my decisions clearer. I've said yes to playing tennis with my daughter. I've said no to watching TV. I've said yes to lunch with my son at school, and I've said no to making sure my house is spotless.

When considering our priorities and our time, an important thing to keep in mind is that we can add the phrase "right now." Having a tidy house is generally a priority for me, but *right now* in this six-month season of manuscript writing and child raising and life living, dishes and laundry have taken a back seat.

There have even been days or weeks when, because of an immediate deadline the next day, I've had to say no to doing things with my family. It doesn't mean that they aren't a priority, but "right now," for a *very brief* moment in time, something else was a temporary priority.

The shifting nature of *urgent* priorities within the grid of *important* priorities is a core concept to grasp. Otherwise, we might always say yes to the two-year-old who wants to play tea party and never cook dinner. There is a very delicate, very fine balance. When we are clear with God and ourselves about what our priorities are, decision-making becomes easier, and our plans for our time begin to align with what is most important to us.

Phase 2: Determine Your Processes

A great example of a process based on a priority is found in something we do every day. We cook. We decide what we want to eat (our priority), then we make a clear plan that will take us from our desire to action: a recipe (our process). Recipes take us step-by-step from choosing our ingredients to assembling them. We start with the vision or priority (our dish) and break it down into processes and practical actions.

Just walking into the kitchen and starting to cook with no end product in mind rarely produces anything anyone wants to eat. But by starting with the end in mind, we are able to use our time effectively *and* efficiently.

To create a recipe, we first need to decide what we're cooking. The same with planning. We need to determine the end product—what we want to do. Where we want to end up. These are our goals. You might not know the ins and outs of your life goals, but I encourage you to start by choosing a few small goals based on your priorities:

- Is faith a priority? What godly characteristics do I want to build into my life?

_____

_____

- Is work a priority? What achievements would advance my career?

_____

_____

- Is community a priority? What is one way I can make a difference where I live?

_____

_____

- Is family a priority? What relationships do I want to improve?

_____

_____

- Is health a priority? What changes do I want to make?

_____

_____

A goal can be small or big. Your goals don't need to be perfect, and, yes, you can tweak them and change them. The goal here is just to set a goal. Work toward something. Author and speaker Zig Ziglar used to say, "If you aim for nothing, you'll hit it every time."[3] There is great effectiveness in stating your goal, your destination.

Now once you have your goal, you need to turn it into a process by simply asking three more questions:

1. How will I measure my goal?
2. When is my deadline for this goal?
3. What action will I take each day to achieve this goal?

For example, if health is one of your priorities and you set the goal of getting more rest, your process could be: Because I care about my health, I will reach my goal of getting more rest this month by going to bed each night at 9:30 p.m. and getting up at 6:30 a.m.

Or if work is a priority and you set the goal of increasing your sales, your process could be: Because my career is a priority, I will increase my sales this quarter by making ten more sales calls each day.

While we can never guarantee a goal will be met, if we set a clear outcome, deadline, and action, we pave the way for success.

It's a beautiful thing to partner with God and work toward a reality that does not yet exist. To work toward the person you have not yet become. To believe and fight for something that will only happen through blood, sweat, and prayers.

Phase 3: Practical Actions

Practical actions simply incorporate our priorities and processes into our daily planning. Let me walk you through my morning *Plan*-time anchor so you can see one way to incorporate bigger-picture goals into your everyday activities. My morning routine starts by reviewing my personal mission statement, which I've written in the present tense so it becomes a sort of prayer:

God, please make these things true of me:
I live each day abiding more and more in God's presence,
　Word, and calling.
I have very strong relationships with Jimmy and each of my
　children, and each one is thriving.
I am fit and well rested for my calling. I am willing to
　follow where He leads.

This process of submitting my mission statement to the Lord becomes a daily alignment check. Is this who I am? Is this who God wants me to be? I never want to be so rigid that my plans take precedence over His.

I then take a few seconds to look at my goals. I have a list of ten life goals. I choose three yearly goals based on those life goals and then I often break the yearly goals down into quarterly goals. That may sound confusing, but the basic idea is like that recipe. I have an idea of what I want to do with my life (my mission statement), and so I use that as my reference to pinpoint my life goals, yearly goals, and then quarterly goals. And finally, I break that down into my daily tasks.

The more our daily tasks line up with our mission statement, the more confident we can be that we are living with integrity.

But what if I don't know my purpose? You might be thinking, *That's great for you, but I have no idea what my purpose is. I don't know what I'd pick for life goals. I don't have a mission statement.*

Don't worry. God has already given you a purpose. We know that we were created for God's glory (Isa. 43:7), and we know we are called to share His love with others (Matt. 28:19). We can always begin each day asking, *how can I bring glory to God today, and how can I be a messenger of His mercy?*

Start there. And as you seek Jesus day by day, read the Word, and deepen your relationship, He will steadily make clear the specific call He has on your life.

Hello Mornings participant Dawna said:

Taking the time to plan has helped me to budget my time. I chunk it out hour by hour so I don't burn out or overcommit. It has relieved so much stress for me. When I see my time as valuable and that it is measurable, then I can make better choices about what I want to spend my time on. Do I want to waste an hour and a half watching a program that I don't really love, or do I want to soak in a bubble bath with a good book? Do I have time to take this phone call right now knowing it will be an hour long when I need to leave for my doctor's appointment in forty-five minutes? Some people may not have a problem with making such decisions, but, for me, I have had to learn how to have good boundaries—and budgeting and blocking out my time hour by hour has really helped me.

I love this advice from Elisa Pulliam:

The best advice I ever heard when it comes to planning and organizing life is this: "If the system you're using doesn't work, change it." That principle has given me freedom to let go of all sorts of failing routines and cumbersome processes in order to create a plan that works in light of my wiring and needs in that season of life.

And if you're in a place in life where the to-do list feels insurmountable, put one foot in front of the other with this advice from life coach Carey Bailey:

When you feel overwhelmed, choose to zoom in on life. Think about what three things you can do in the next two hours, and discover your focus in the few things that can get done rather than the pile that feels impossible.

The Impact of *Plan* Time

Remember to tie your priorities, process, and practical application all back to the morning anchor with this question: *Am I consistent in submitting my plans to God?* This is a time to review where we feel God is leading, remember our plans for the day, and surrender it all to Him afresh so our plans never become an idol of accomplishment.

If we want to live effectively, there is no better way than to submit our time and plans to God. That will look different for different personalities in different seasons of life. The key for you is to understand how God made you, where He's leading you, and how you can best get there.

seven

Move Time

With three kids in three different schools that start at three different times, as well as a cornucopia of other extracurricular activities, it's not unusual for me to spend three hours a day in my car. I guess you could say I'm more of a stay-in-car mom than a stay-at-home mom. Most of those hours in my car are spent driving within four miles of my house. My house that I miss very much.

I spend the rest of my stay-in-car time waiting. There's lots of waiting. So as we sit in the high school car line for my oldest, Anna, my two younger kids and I sometimes play the "Which team is that?" game. The school's massive Texas-sized athletic complex sits across the parking lot from the main education building. The teams walk past us to after-school practice, and we try to guess their sport before we can read it on their shirts.

"Soccer!"

"That one is definitely football!"

"Softball!"

"Cross-country!"

It's fascinating how you can often identify a team's sport by the kids' body types (not always, of course). The smaller, leaner athletes are cross-country runners. The tall athletes with strong shoulders are basketball or volleyball players. Muscular legs and a lean frame usually point to soccer or tennis. Strong bodies and a compact frame are often baseball or softball. A tall, large, hulking frame is either football or someone the football coach is desperately trying to recruit.

Of course, there are always outliers whose athletic abilities aren't affected by their build, but, in general, different sports clearly benefit from different physical attributes. Wouldn't it be silly if a golfer spent his time trying to add bulk like a linebacker? Or if a soccer player focused on arm strength like a baseball player? That would be pointless. Athletes base their workouts on their pursuit of excellence on the field, not on how they look.

Shift Your *Move*-Time Perspective

What if we've been thinking about fitness all wrong? What if it has nothing to do with a number on a scale or a size on a tag? What if it has nothing to do with how much we can lift or how far we can run? What if those are all just vanity metrics—misleading indicators of our true health?

Shift 1: Fitness Is About Energy, Not Image

I wonder if this bit of sports trivia could also be true for us. Just as successful athletes come in all shapes and sizes tailored to their sport, maybe we are not all meant to look exactly the same because we do not all have the same God-given purpose.

Contrary to what the fitness industry tries to tell me, I don't need six-pack abs to be an effective author or a great mom to my three kids. But Jennie Finch, who is also a mother of three, probably needed six-pack abs to pitch the USA national softball team to multiple Olympic medals.

The thirty-one-year-old first-grade teacher requires different energy, focus, and fitness levels than the fifty-five-year-old empty-nester accountant. The sixteen-year-old Olympic gymnast has different strength needs than the eighteen-year-old painter. And the eighty-year-old grandmother requires different endurance than a twenty-five-year-old young mother of quadruplets.

I don't know about you, but I want to be ready and able to step into God's story. If there is a need, I want to be first in line to say, "Here I am. Send me!" (Isa. 6:8).

God doesn't want us to simply read His Word and go about our days. He wants His Word to infiltrate every area of our lives. He wants us not only to marinate in its truth but also to let it influence our daily plans and actions.

Perhaps after you read about the feeding of the five thousand (Mark 6:30–44) during your Bible study, God will lead you to cook a meal for a neighbor. Or after reading about the widow's mite (Luke 21:1–4), you'll be moved to mow a widow's yard or do some chores around her home. Maybe God will want you to walk in greater patience and faith as a mother or memorize a large passage of Scripture. Maybe He'll want you to coach a local youth sports team or join a running group to get to know new people. Maybe He'll ask you to travel overseas to serve refugees. Or maybe He'll ask you to move to another city or country to serve others there.

But how can we be ready? That's what Hello Mornings is all about. *God. Plan. Move.*

Shift 2: It's Not About How We Look but How We Live

We prepare ourselves by studying God's Word (*God* time), we plan our days according to His leading (*Plan* time), but we also need the energy to do as He asks (*Move* time).

So while you might have thought of *Move* time as working out, I'd like to propose a radical shift in how we think about exercise and fitness. It's not just sweating, dieting, and basically suffering in some form or fashion with the goal of changing our physical strength or appearance. When that is our goal, fitness is only about image. *How do I look? How much do I weigh? What size do I wear? How strong am I? Who can I impress with the way I look?* Essentially, *How can I bring glory to myself through my body?*

I wonder if, as believers, we might claim a different perspective—one that frees us from a one-size-fits-all standard and offers a grace that moves us forward.

God's ultimate purpose for our physical bodies isn't based on how we look in a bathing suit or how much we weigh. It isn't even about how we feel about ourselves or the example we leave for our children. Those might all be lovely by-products of being healthy, but, as believers, the sole purpose of our fitness is to answer this one question: *Am I fit enough to do all God has called me to do with excellence and joy in this season of my life?*

Here are some questions to help you evaluate your answer:

- Do I have the energy to be patient with my loved ones—even at 3:00 p.m., 5:00 p.m., or 8:00 p.m.?

- Do I have the focus in the morning to start work and stay on task?
- Are any of my choices keeping me from having the energy to serve and invest in others?
- Do my comfort and security come from God, food, or my fitness level?
- Am I energetic enough to build relationships with friends when they invite me to do things with them?
- Is how I treat my body helping me to excel at what God has called me to do in this season, or is it hindering me?

If we can grasp the concept that fitness is not about image but about energy, it changes so much of what we think about our health. This perspective shift is huge. As believers, we look at the world through the lens of our faith. Why should our health be any different? We are to be doers of the word and not just hearers. We want our faith to take action in our everyday lives. So the question we ask ourselves is this: *How am I managing my energy so I'm living my days in the way God intended?*

There may be strangers you're supposed to encourage today. There may be friends you're supposed to serve. There may be family members who need you to be their strength. Are you missing the miracles God has for you and others because you're just too tired?

I confess I've typically thought about fitness in terms of weight, clothing size, or how I looked. But in God's upside-down kingdom, He measures things differently. The internal comes before the external.

Being fit in this way is actually a lot like being an elite

athlete. Olympians don't work out to look good. In fact, they might work out less or differently if looks were their primary motivation. Instead, their main goal is to perform with excellence and to represent their country well. Being fit is simply a by-product of their faithful dedication.

We should have a similar perspective. Our health affects so much more than just how we look. It affects how we feel, how we act, the decisions we make, and our ability to focus and succeed at the opportunities God has given us. Let's shift our primary motivation for fitness. Let's focus on building our energy to serve rather than building our image to impress.

Will you take a moment to answer this question right now? *Am I fit enough to do all that God has called me to do in this season of my life with excellence and joy?*

Whether your answer is yes or no, be encouraged. With this fresh perspective, you'll find transformation easier than ever.

Set Your *Move*-Time Anchor

Frankly, when the focus of fitness is image, change is hard to come by. We want to see results quickly—and when we stop seeing results, we get discouraged. Fast results require enormous effort and self-discipline, and we just can't keep that up.

Energy, however, can change overnight. (Literally. You'll see what I mean later in this chapter.) So how do we make ourselves "fit" for what God has in store for us each day?

Just as with our *God* time and *Plan* time, we also should have a *Move*-time anchor—a healthy choice we can make every day, no matter what. It's our stake in the ground saying,

No matter what today holds, I'm going to start well and lay claim to my health.

In our Hello Mornings three-minute morning challenge, we start with our *God*-time anchor (praying Psalm 143:8), then our *Plan*-time anchor (prayerfully reviewing our calendars), and finally our *Move*-time anchor (drinking a glass of water). You'll see how important water is in just a minute. The beauty is that we can do all this in about three minutes. I keep water on my nightstand and at my desk, so no matter how or where I start my morning, I have everything I need.

Again, the three-minute morning routine is simply a foundation for you. Feel free to mix it up and pick a different simple habit that fits your situation and personality best.

Here are some other one-minute actions you can take:

- Drink a cup of warm herbal tea (bonus if you add lemon).
- Do a small exercise (just one minute—remember the goal is to make this something you can do every single day without willpower). Perhaps do a plank, jumping jacks, push-ups, sit-ups, but only do these if you enjoy them. Make sure your *Move* habit is a launching pad and not a stumbling block.
- Decide on your healthy meals for the day, and evaluate what you ate yesterday.
- Stretch.

I can't emphasize enough that this morning *Move* habit is about faithful consistency, not the effectiveness of the workout or pushing yourself. Do not make this hard. Make it easy. Make it consistent. And then build on it.

If you want to do something other than drink a glass of water, what will be your *Move*-time anchor?

_____

_____

_____

Once you have your *Move* habit down, you'll want to increase your energy through fitness. Let's talk about how to do that effectively. I'll give you a clue: it doesn't start with a ninety-minute workout DVD or going on an intense diet. I know that's normally where we start when we think of fitness, but the fact is, the harder it is to reach a goal, the harder it will be to maintain that level of fitness. There's no use in trying to sprint a marathon; we'll only burn out. Our efforts toward better health must start with simple, consistent habits. Slow and steady wins the race.

Start Growing Your *Move* Time

I can be a bit competitive. In fact, I'm so competitive that I don't even need someone else to compete against. Last week as I was cleaning off my desk in preparation to write, I crumpled up a scratch piece of paper and threw it into a trash can across the room.

I missed.

Obviously that was an affront to my athletic ability, so I now *had* to make the shot. For the next fifteen minutes, I shot that piece of paper, missed, walked over, picked it up, sat back down in my chair, shot, missed, walked over, picked it up, sat back down in my chair, shot, missed . . . you get the idea.

I wasted fifteen minutes of writing time. Why? All I wanted was a clean desk. I could have simply stood up, walked over, and *placed* the paper in the trash can. I am ridiculous.

How often, though, do we do the same thing with our health?

We put all our energy into "one shot"—banking our health on a single exhaustive exercise routine or diet solution that requires all our focus and willpower. We try and fail again and again with these quick fixes when we could just take small, sure steps.

This is why fitness seems difficult. No matter how hard we try, we can't undo in thirty days what we've spent a lifetime building. If the decline of our health didn't happen overnight, we can't expect to fix it overnight. So while a "Thirty-Day Fix" or a "Twenty-One-Day Cleanse" may give us a jump-start, these things cannot be the foundation of our health.

Where do we begin the process of growing our energy? The easiest way to grow your move time is by focusing on three things.

STEP 1. TRACK

Start noticing different aspects of your health. Your *sleep, hydration, nutrition,* and *exercise.* Noticing is far more powerful than we think.

STEP 2. TRADE

Make simple swaps. If we take just a little time to try new things, we'll discover that we can make enormous healthy changes that require zero willpower.

STEP 3. TRY

This is where people usually start. They try to do the hard things first and burn out. Instead, save this for last, and try hard things in small spurts, knowing you can always fall back on your core habit.

The beauty of tracking your health is that you don't need to do anything traditionally associated with fitness, such as dieting, cardio, or weights. You'll be amazed at how effective it is to simply notice what you are already doing in a few key areas. You'll begin to see that your body may already be telling you where to start. Is your body letting you know it's tired? Or thirsty? Or in need of better nutrition? When we shift our perspective on fitness from image to energy, we change the starting point. So instead of starting with exercise, start with your energy source.

Your energy comes from three main sources: sleep, hydration, and nutrition. We'll begin with these essential building blocks, tracking our habits and trading where necessary as we try new things.

And, by the way, I don't know about you, but I am *all in* on a fitness plan that starts with more sleep.

Sleep

My friend Kristiana and her husband, Eric, had a rough time after their son Jack was born. The sleep deprivation hit both of them hard, but the impact on Eric, a very intelligent and levelheaded man, has become legendary. He was so tired he would often wake up in the middle of the night speaking or acting illogically about where the baby was or how he was doing.

One night Kristiana woke up to see Eric cradling a partially open package of toilet paper. Somehow, he mistook the Charmin for baby Jack. As he comforted their "baby," one of the rolls of toilet paper fell out of the top opening, and Eric started yelling, "His head fell off! His head fell off! Kristiana, his head fell off!"

Desperately trying to hold back her laughter, Kristiana roused her husband out of his delirium and showed him their son was peacefully sleeping in his crib . . . with his head securely in place.

Sleep, or lack thereof, has a profound impact on our well-being—and sanity. We tend to treat our bodies as if they are bionic and will never break, but many of us have found out the hard way that is the furthest thing from the truth. Not only can lack of sleep make us loopy or cranky, studies show it can actually impair our responses to a degree on par with being legally drunk.[1] (I think toilet-paper Jack can attest to that.)

If we want to maximize our energy so we can follow wherever God may lead, we must start with sleep. Are we getting enough? Are we consistent with our sleep schedule? Are we getting quality sleep?

Quality sleep impacts every area of our well-being and has been linked to reducing high blood pressure, lowering cholesterol, more effective learning, and a stronger immune system.[2] Bottom line: we may treat sleep as if it's optional, but it is essential. To sacrifice sleep for anything is truly a sacrifice. If you want to maximize your energy, this is the place to start.

Let's begin by answering some questions:

* Am I getting enough sleep?

_____

_____

* Is my sleep consistent?

_____

_____

* Am I getting quality sleep?

_____

_____

* What can I do to improve my rest?

_____

_____

Here are a few simple ways to improve your sleep.

STEP 1: TRACK

* Prioritize getting your optimal amount of sleep. For most people this is seven to eight hours per night.
* Wear a tracker like a Fitbit or a smart watch to evaluate how restful or restless your sleep is. There are even phone apps that can help you track your sleep.

STEP 2: TRADE

It's harder to find the time to get *more* sleep than it is to get *better* sleep. So before we tackle the challenge of increasing our sleep, let's first trade in some bad sleep habits for better ones.

- Turn off your phone an hour before bed. The blue light emitted from digital devices tricks our bodies into believing it's still daylight and delays our normal nighttime release of melatonin, a chemical that calms us down and prepares us for quality sleep.[3]
- Keep it cold. Experts suggest 65 to 72 degrees to be optimal.[4]
- Keep it dark.[5]

STEP 3: TRY

Finally, it's time to figure out why you aren't getting enough sleep. Whether you're losing sleep because you're staying up too late or getting up too early, review your sleep patterns, and figure out how you can trade some evening or morning time to get a sufficient amount of rest.

It might be that you're staying up late to work or study or "relax." Or maybe you're getting up early to work out. When it comes to our morning workout, it's important not to fall into the trap of getting up earlier without *also* going to bed earlier.

Well-known fitness blogger and instructor Clare Smith says, "The key to a simple morning is having an effective night before! Set out your workout clothes, music player, water bottle, and keys (if you are leaving the house), and know what workout you are going to do."

According to research, getting up an hour earlier to work out may not be very effective for some people. A recent study in the *Annals of Internal Medicine* revealed that getting less sleep (5.5 hours versus 8.5 hours per night) decreases how much fat our bodies use for energy and increases the use of fat-free body mass, like carbohydrates and protein for energy.[6] Meaning, our bodies burn less fat and, instead, burn nutrients we need for strong, lean bodies. Sleep aids the effectiveness of our exercise.

For some of you, though, sufficient rest just isn't a possibility right now. I'm looking at you, new parents—or perhaps those of you working multiple jobs. After a long day, all we want is to relax; but in challenging seasons that threaten our sleep, it's worth it to choose sleep over a favorite TV show or scrolling through social media. Ask yourself, *What is one simple thing I can do to improve my sleep?*

Hydration

Did you know that the human body is 60 percent water? We've all heard we should drink eight glasses a day, but few of us consistently drink as much water as our bodies optimally require. In fact, one study revealed that more than half of the children in the United States are chronically dehydrated. Dehydration not only influences our current mood but also can lead to increased blood pressure, higher cholesterol, and decreased energy levels.[7]

Drinking more water is the quickest, simplest way we can scale up our energy.

The interesting thing about the human body is that it doesn't care how it gets water. So we often confuse thirst with hunger. While food can provide as much as 20 percent of our water intake, it's easy to overeat when all we need is a drink. Staying hydrated wards off the mindless snacking that leads to poor food choices and energy crashes.

So how can we consistently drink enough to operate at our optimum level?

STEP 1: TRACK

You can track your water intake with an app. Or a lower-tech idea is to wear several bangle bracelets and move them from one arm to the other as you finish a glass so you have a visual of how well you've hydrated your body that day.

STEP 2: TRADE

Trade your first drink of the day for water. Clare Smith suggests, "Drink 8–16 ounces of water before you have your coffee." You can always have your coffee or tea right after, but starting with that first glass starts you off on the right foot. Trade your soda or sweet tea at restaurants for lemon water. While sodas and other drinks hydrate you to some degree, most contain caffeine, which is a diuretic, causing you to lose most of that liquid via more frequent trips to the bathroom.

STEP 3: TRY

After you have the habit of starting your day with water and keeping track of how much you're drinking, consider trying a new habit of carrying a water bottle around or replacing your soda consumption with water.

Keep water bottles in your car and at your desk. Keep a collapsible cup in your purse, and get in the habit of always ordering water with your meal, along with any other drink you may order.

You've probably heard these ideas before, but the key here is to remember our *why*. We drink more water not because some doctor or magazine article or book said we should. We do it because we want to be ready at every moment for whatever God may bring our way.

We want to make these small, simple choices because they make us ready for big, difficult choices. We want to steward well the body God has given us and make it ready to do good works. "Whoever can be trusted with very little can also be trusted with much" (Luke 16:10).

Sleep more. Drink water. This fitness thing is easy!

Ask yourself, *What is one simple thing I can do to improve my hydration?*

_____

_____

Nutrition

Remember when I said fitness doesn't have to be hard? It really doesn't. You don't even need to start improving your nutrition by dieting. In fact, I don't recommend it.

Why? Well, because dieting *is* hard. It's time-consuming, and most people don't like it. We are pursuing lifelong change. We want to build consistent habits. We aren't sprinting marathons.

In fact, did you know that the word *marathon* comes from the legend of Pheidippides who ran from Marathon to Athens to announce the Greek victory in the Battle of Marathon? The legend says he ran the entire way, all twenty-five miles . . . and then, after delivering the message, he collapsed and died.[8] Don't try to sprint a marathon. Pace yourself.

STEP 1: TRACK

When we talk about nutrition, we need to ask ourselves one key question: *Is this energy food or entertainment food?* We eat some things to give us energy, and we eat other things for entertainment. Ice cream is an entertainment food. Spinach is an energy food. Pizza is entertainment food. Broccoli is energy food. A bacon cheeseburger is entertainment food. Grilled salmon is energy food.

Once you start asking the energy-or-entertainment question, you'll find you naturally begin to make different choices. The sheer act of noticing inspires us to make wiser decisions. I love how Revelation Wellness founder Alisa Keeton put it: "Set your mind to make food and fitness decisions based on what would be good and kind to your body. Your body is not the enemy. And neither is food."

STEP 2: TRADE

We often think of nutrition as dieting, restricting ourselves from foods we like, and only eating weird things we can't pronounce. But God made a whole world of delicious things to eat. Trade a burger for a high-quality chicken sandwich. Trade out a bag of candy for gum. Trade out a Snickers for a chocolate-chip granola bar.

There are so many good options that are also helpful for our bodies. Take the time to swap out one food each week. You'll be amazed at how you can seamlessly eliminate a fatty, sugary, energy-draining food for a healthy snack without actually sacrificing the entertainment value. Chili is a good example of a win-win food (assuming you like chili, which I do). Hummus is another good one. My favorite burger place offers a lettuce-wrapped burger that I truly enjoy every bit as much as the one with bread. It's an easy trade, but I probably would forget about it if I didn't keep a list on my phone of my favorite healthy options at different restaurants. As we identify foods that are good for both entertainment and energy, healthy eating becomes our new norm.

STEP 3: TRY

After you've built the habit of tracking what you eat and trading out a few entertainment foods for energy foods, it's time to try a challenge.

Add green smoothies to your daily menu. Try kale. Do a juice cleanse.

Find a way to challenge yourself to broaden your palate and make nutritional choices based on energy and not just taste.

If you consistently repeat this process—track, trade, and try—you'll transform your eating habits without much effort and improve your health from the inside out.

Watch your energy rise, and get excited about the foundation of healthy living that you're building. Ask yourself, *What is one simple thing I can do to improve my nutrition?*

_____

_____

Exercise

Once you have your sleep, hydration, and nutrition rolling along, it's time to build on that with strength and endurance.

Again, this doesn't have to be hard. I'm not talking about signing up for the next Ironman. If we have a long-term perspective, we are less likely to overdo things that lead to burnout. Even just a couple minutes in the morning can lead to an internal and external transformation.

The world of exercise can be overwhelming. It is a billion-dollar-a-year industry with more workout programs and training plans than you could complete in a lifetime. So where do we start?

The first place to start is where we've started before. Noticing. Just as it's important to notice how we are sleeping, drinking, and eating, the first step is to notice how much or little we are moving.

STEP 1: TRACK

Are you on your feet all day? Or is your day filled with sitting at work, in the car, or on the couch?

When my husband and I started changing our movement level, our kids thought we'd officially gone crazy. We were helping them with their homework, cooking, and watching TV while walking in circles through our kitchen, dining room, and living room. Jimmy and I had just gotten fitness trackers, and let's just say we're a little competitive. Determined to outstep one another, we spontaneously jogged in place, briskly lapped our house while brushing our teeth, and generally acted like crazy people. Not only was it good for our bodies and inspiring (or embarrassing) for the kids, but it was also fun for us. We doubled the amount of exercise we were getting without doing anything difficult. We just noticed and had fun.

You might be surprised by how little movement (or maybe how much) you get. This is where a fitness tracker or pedometer can be helpful. Without any extra effort, you can track your movement—*and* most fitness trackers also monitor your sleep and allow you to keep track of your water as well.

STEP 2: TRADE

Now it's time to make some trades. What are some simple changes you can make to consistently add more movement into your day? Park farther away at the store. Walk your dog instead of just taking him to the dog park and sitting. Take the stairs instead of the elevator. Go for a walk after dinner instead of sitting down to watch TV.

STEP 3: TRY

Experiment with different forms of exercise, and find one you like. Maybe it's running, skating, lifting weights, or biking. Maybe you like tennis or a few bodyweight exercises throughout the day like push-ups or sit-ups.

The goal is to find something that you want to do, that you can do, and that will fit in your schedule. So if you like tennis, but you're busy, try hitting a ball against the side of your house for a quick workout. Don't have time to head to the gym to lift weights? Get a weight set you can use at home or a chin-up bar.

No matter how much we grow in our daily exercise routine, it's important that we always continue our core morning *Move*-time anchor. Exercise builds our strength and endurance and allows us to live and follow God with more energy, excellence, and joy.

Ask yourself, *What is one simple thing I can do to improve my exercise routine?*

_____

_____

The Impact of *Move* Time

What does all this have to do with morning routines? As you consider what our *Move* time means, I want you to feel the freedom to be creative with how you use that time. It might be reviewing what you ate yesterday or planning what you'll eat today. It might be making a quick, energy-filled breakfast or putting food in the Crock-Pot for a healthy dinner.

By changing our definition of fitness, we break the chains of perfection. We move the focus of our efforts from the end results to daily progress. And we build our confidence that our optimum energy level is the goal regardless of whether the shape on the outside will fit the high standards of our society.

By building our morning core habit, we remind ourselves day in and day out of our priorities.

The point of *Move* time isn't simply to increase our energy; it's to increase our energy *so* we can best respond to God's call in our lives each day. Are we moving through our day with open and responsive hearts ready to serve others, pray, give, and love as God calls us to?

Are we hearing the Word *and* doing it? How can we maintain an open posture before God throughout our day, and how can we overcome our fears and step outside of our comfort zones and our routines to follow wherever God may lead? As we increase our energy, are we asking God what more we can do for and with Him? This isn't about settling into our comfort zones; it's about excelling in the role God has given us.

Your *Move* time doesn't need to involve a treadmill or the gym. It just needs to focus on building your energy to follow God whenever and wherever He may lead.

Whatever emotions you've had in the past about your health or your body, now is the time to lay those at the feet of Jesus. The beauty of integrating our *God* time, *Plan* time, and *Move* time is that we can move into each segment with increasing freedom. When we surround our exercise time with *God* time, we insulate ourselves from the many messages the Enemy uses to discourage and disconnect us.

As part of your *God* time, lay your fears and insecurities before the One who designed every part of you. In faith, believe that you are wholly designed for the glory of God and to bring hope to others. He made you the way you are for a reason. As you pursue your optimal energy level, don't believe the lie that you need to fit into a box or be like anyone else. When you run someone else's race, you leave a void in the race you are supposed to run (Heb. 12:1).

Our God is not a redundant Creator. It's time to start running *your* race.

part three

Your Morning Routine Toolkit

eight

How to Build Habits

It usually happens between 9:30 p.m. and 11:00 p.m.

"I'm heading to bed." I'm always startled by his announcement because, normally, if anyone goes to bed early, it's me. But on rare occasions, my husband, Jimmy, will make this announcement first, and my brain has one of two responses. The first is, *Oh no! I was going to go to bed early. If I don't get up now before he leaves the room, I'm doomed. Dr. Jekyll-Kat will take over.*

My other response is, *Yes! Get thee to bed! I get the house to myself! Solitude! Quiet! Introvert party time!*

Since both Jimmy and I work from home, and we have three children (one of whom I homeschool), I'm rarely alone. So there's something magical about sitting in a quiet house when everyone is sleeping.

The world is my oyster!

I can do *whatever* I want.

No one is going to talk to me for a *whole* eight hours.

It's almost like I'm in college again, and I completely forget the reality that I have to wake up at 5:30 a.m., and life is still going to happen.

But in that blissful realization that I have "unending solitude," I forget every practicality and descend into my suburban-mom-frat-party mode. Soon, cans of sparkling water and veggie chip bags are strewn all around me as I lay sprawled on the couch, iPad on my stomach, watching some variation of a Jane Austen book turned movie.

When my supply of healthy snacks runs out, I head back to the kitchen to scrounge for any unhealthy food I can find. Usually the pickings are slim, but there are glorious times when a carton of mint chocolate-chip ice cream is in the freezer, and all my dreams come true.

Having squished as many scoops as humanly possible into my *small* bowl, I snuggle under a blanket back on the couch and proceed to waste hours upon hours watching incredibly cheesy movies while filling my stomach with food I don't need. And I love every minute . . . until the self-loathing begins: *Wait. What! Two a.m.? How can it be two a.m.?! It was just nine forty-five p.m.! What have I even been doing the past [counts on fingers] four hours? I'm going to be worthless tomorrow!*

My sparkling water, veggie crisp, Jane Austen binge finally comes to a screeching halt when my forty-year-old body declares bankruptcy and refuses to support my eyelids, and I nod off.

I know it's bad for me. I know I shouldn't do it. I know I'll have a terrible day the next day. But it's become a habit.

When I'm left alone in the living room late at night, all my cravings cue up (*Mindless surfing! Snacks! Miss Bennet and Mr. Darcy!*); I descend, almost against my will, into my routine.

What about you? Maybe it's not staying up late or binge

eating your favorite ice cream, but do you have a habit you *know* is bad, but you find yourself doing anyway? Maybe it's ordering a soda or grabbing a morning doughnut. Maybe it's driving too fast or procrastinating when you feel overwhelmed.

Why do we develop these habits that we don't really want? And how can we harness whatever is powering them and turn it into something good?

Is that even possible?

As we work to build morning routines of *God* time, *Plan* time, and *Move* time, we need to utilize the power of habit to create a lifelong change. Charles Duhigg, the author of the *New York Times* bestselling book *The Power of Habit*, says that a habit consists of three elements: a cue, a routine, and a reward.[1] In my case, the cue was being alone in the living room. The routine was grabbing suburban-mom junk food and hitting play on a cheesy movie. And the reward was feeling like I was a carefree twenty-year-old again. According to Duke University researchers, nearly 40 percent of what we do every day is a product of habit rather than conscious decision.[2]

If you think about it, you'll begin to recognize all the habitual moments in your day: The way you brush your teeth, how you drive to work, the order in which you get dressed or make your breakfast. Tying your shoes. Checking your phone. These are all habits.

Shift Your Habit-Building Perspective

Have you ever seen a baby learn to walk? One hundred percent of their baby attention is on the task. Babies don't learn to walk while texting on their toy phones or reading the *New York Times*. They just focus on walking.

Why? Everything new requires significantly more attention from our bodies and brains.

God made our brains to be automation machines. Whenever we learn something new, there's a little middle manager guy in our brain saying, "Hey! Can we automate this? How can we automate this? How about now? Can we automate it now?" He's just itching to make a habit out of everything we do because God made our brains to pursue efficiency.

When we learn something new, a part of our brain called the cerebrum is on full alert. It's working overtime to process the new information, understand patterns, and master the skill. But as we repeat it over and over, all that processing power moves to the area of our brain called the basal ganglia—this is where our more subconscious activities are managed: things such as breathing, blinking, walking, and brushing our teeth.[3] We don't think about *how* to do these things. They are automated. They're habits.

Habits allow our conscious brains to free up space by transferring the command center for that activity to the subconscious part of the brain, allowing us to then master new tasks while still performing the old ones.

Think about how hard it was for you to drive to the grocery store the first time you moved to a new town. *Do I turn here? Or here? Was it on the left or right? Did I just pass it?*

Now you probably think about a million other things on the way to the grocery store. You don't consciously remind yourself how to get there, so your brain is free to solve new problems.

This is why you can accomplish so much more at once as an adult than you could as a child. You can walk and talk and be aware of your surroundings. You can read quickly and write easily. Habits are wonderful and powerful tools.

But habits aren't just passive by-products of repetition. We can purposefully develop and form habits of our choosing as well. This is how athletes become so highly skilled. They use their conscious brains to learn a skill, turn the skill into a habit, send it to their subconscious brains, and then free up space to learn another new skill.

Habits are the building blocks of excellence.

Set Your Habit-Building Anchor

Habits are stepping-stones to get you to a destination. You can build them, add to them, and use them over and over again to get where you want to go.

Last spring my family went for a hike only to find that the recent rains made for a very messy adventure. We came to a particularly muddy spot in the river, and one by one my family members tried to jump across—and invariably landed in the sticky mud. Not wanting to have to clean my shoes, I took a large rock from the river and put it down in the mud. Then I got another large rock and stood on the first stone and put the second one farther along in the mud.

It took longer and required a little extra effort, but my shoes stayed dry; and on the way back, everyone in my family avoided the mud by walking on the rocks I'd placed.

Building habits in our lives is like placing those rocks in

the mud. Once they're in place, we can rely on them. We can add to them, and others can learn from and trust in them.

They are a foundation.

You've probably heard the Bible story of the man who built his house on rock and the other man who built his house on sand (Matt. 7:24–27). No doubt the sand guy got the job done faster. It's easier to move sand into place. He was probably sipping lemonade in the sun while the rock guy was schlepping rocks into place.

But in the long run, only one house stood.

Habits are a strong foundation, and the more good habits we build, the better off we are.

Do you brush your teeth every day? Would it be hard for you to *not* brush your teeth before bed? It's a habit. And good or bad, habits are hard to break.

How would it feel if, a year from now, it seemed weird *not* to work out every day? What if you just couldn't start your day without Jesus? What if planning your day in a way that brought peace and clarity was just the "thing you did" each day?

How would that affect your life? How would you feel if you could stop feeling guilty about *not* doing these things but, instead, *always* did them?

It would feel . . . awesome!

Start Growing Your Habit Building

But how do we build habits? We build them slowly and steadily. It's a bit like pushing a car in neutral down a decline. Starting takes focus and effort, but soon enough it will roll on by itself, and take you along for the ride.

Before we dive into the details of habit building, right out of the gate I'd like to address two common misconceptions about habits.

The first one is that we must do it all, and do it perfectly, from the minute we start. We become kamikaze habit builders, diving in fast and deep, trying to build a habit way out of our comfort zone and ultimately crashing and burning. There are steps to creating habits. Shortcuts don't usually serve anyone well.

The second misconception is that habit building must begin with self-discipline and willpower. But, in reality, those should be our last-ditch resources. There are *much* easier ways to start our habit building. Let me introduce you to seven of my favorite tools.

Tool 1: Triggers

Triggers are probably the most powerful habit-building tools. I used a trigger to get back in the routine of working out at the gym. You see, during the school year, I follow the same routine every single school day: wake up, do my morning routine, wake the kids, get ready, say good-bye to my oldest as she waits for her carpool, take the carpool kids to one school, and then drop my son off at his school. Rinse, wash, repeat. Same every morning. We almost have it all down to a science. It's a habit.

It's been a few years since I've consistently gone to the gym, and as much as I like running and working out at home, I know that I push myself harder and can be more consistent at the gym because weather doesn't impact my workout.

So when school started up this year, I thought it would be a great time to get back into going to the gym. And since it is located at my son's school, what better way to build the habit than to tack it on to our current morning routine?

My trigger is that I'm already at the school, so I just drive around to the back, park, and head to the gym. This is an example of choice architecture (the next tool we discuss). I intentionally drop off my son last so it's a no-brainer decision to go to the gym.

A trigger for you could be your morning alarm, brushing your teeth, taking a shower, or going to bed. It could be mealtime or getting in the car.

My son has to memorize Bible verses for school, and his trigger to work on his memory verse is taking a shower. He tapes his verse to the outside of our glass shower door, and he works on his verse during his shower.

You can also use emotions as triggers. When I'm feeling frustrated or overwhelmed during the workday, that's a trigger for me to go for a walk.

When one of my kids is upset, we'll soon hear music floating through the house, as high emotions are a trigger for that child to practice his or her instrument.

If you're feeling tired, that can be a trigger for you to drink water.

The key here is to simply be aware, have a habit script, and use choice architecture (our next tool) to help you build healthy habits.

Tool 2: Choice Architecture

My favorite way to build a habit requires zero willpower or self-discipline. It's called choice architecture. That means organizing our environment to make it easier to make a particular choice. It's what grocery stores do to sell more of certain items. They place those items at eye level or at the front of the store. We can use this same method to help us build better habits.

Anne Thorndike performed a study at the Massachusetts General Hospital cafeteria that showed how awareness and placement of healthy options at the hospital cafeteria impacted the choices people made.

Thorndike and her team performed this study in two phases. In phase one of studying choice architecture, they used a labeling system to make customers aware of the health value of the items they purchased. Red meant unhealthy, yellow meant less healthy, and green meant healthy. And in phase two of studying choice architecture, they moved the healthy items to the most visible, convenient locations in the cafeteria.

After three months, sales of unhealthy beverages dropped by more than 29 percent, and sales of water increased by more than 25 percent.[4] No one had to use willpower. No one was told to make healthier choices. Thorndike and her team simply labeled and rearranged, and they saw a significant change in customers' habits.

How can you apply choice architecture to your mornings? It might be as simple as putting all your morning supplies, such as your journal, Bible, and pen, into a basket so you can wake up and get started. Maybe it involves gathering all the Bibles you have and placing them in key spots around your home. Maybe it's buying a fitness tracker so you're aware of how much you're moving throughout the day.

Whatever habit you want to focus on, a key step to building

it is to use choice architecture to create an environment that helps you make the choices you truly want to make each day.

Tool 3: Tiny Habits

The next step is to start small. Crazy small. In fact, Stanford University professor and habit expert Dr. B. J. Fogg calls them *tiny habits*. He encourages his students to begin a new habit with a step so small that you can't possibly skip it because it's too hard or time-consuming. His example is for students who want to build the habit of flossing their teeth. His recommendation? Start by committing to floss *one tooth* each night.[5]

Remember, we want our willpower to be our last defense. We want to build a baseline that doesn't require self-discipline.

But one tooth? I know it sounds ridiculous. But the fact is the New Year's resolution approach of massive change all at once doesn't work for most people. So why not try something new?

Dr. Fogg's research and years of teaching have proven that the tiny-habits method is extremely effective.[6] A tiny habit that is truly too easy to quit also helps reveal the true obstacles that keep someone from moving forward.

If you get off track with a tiny habit, you immediately know that it wasn't because it was too difficult. Maybe it was a habit you feel you "should" do or that someone else expects of you. Maybe you're too busy or distracted. Maybe you need to work on other foundational habits first.

With habits broken down into such small steps, you can be sure they alone aren't the reason you're quitting. The smaller the changes you make, the easier it is to accurately identify the obstacles keeping you from long-term change.

What does this look like for a morning routine?

Let's break it down into ridiculously little steps, as if we are teaching space aliens what they need to do:

1. Set alarm before getting into bed.
2. Turn off alarm when it rings.
3. Get out of bed.
4. Brush your teeth.
5. Get dressed.
6. Make a pot of coffee.
7. Drink coffee.
8. Read Bible and pray.
9. Do a one-minute plank.
10. Write down three things that need to happen today.
11. Write down how long each should take.
12. Write down *when* the three things will get done.
13. Take a goofy or unflattering picture.
14. Text a friend the goofy picture so she can post it to social media if the steps don't get done.

Work on one tiny habit each week and share it with someone. For one week, make setting your alarm a little early your focus, until you're itching to move on. Then set the alarm, and make getting out of bed your tiny habit for the next week. And, yes, all you need to do is set your alarm and get out of bed. You can get right back in if you want to. Crazy, I know. But try it. You'll actually love it. Having the willpower to get out but then knowing you can get right back in guilt-free is awesome.

Instead of committing to go to the gym for an hour a day (when you haven't been exercising at all and don't even recall where the gym is located), try committing to laying out your workout clothes for a full week, putting one on each morning, and doing one plank for a minute. Get in the habit of working out before taking on a huge commitment to something you've never even done before.

But will these tiny habits actually get you anywhere?

When I was pregnant with my son Jackson, I decided I wanted to run a half marathon in the next year. Now, I'd never run in anything that ended with "thon." I'd never even run more than a single-digit distance, and being about nine months pregnant, I certainly hadn't run in quite a while.

It was a rather ridiculous goal. Pregnancy, newborns, and training for long-distance races don't mesh. But I knew it was something I wanted to do. I decided right there in my living room to start training. And I did that by getting up to get my *own* ice cream instead of pulling the pregnant-wife card and asking my husband to get it for me.

That's right: my training for a race titled "the hardest half in Texas" started with ice cream.

It sounds silly, but I made a series of choices and took small steps toward my goal. In his 1913 autobiography, Theodore Roosevelt shared a powerful quote from William Meek "Squire Bill" Widener: "Do what you can, with what you've got, where you are."[7]

Eventually, I upgraded from a walk to the fridge to walking around the block. My first post-birth run was ugly. I'm pretty sure things were moving that weren't supposed to move. I made it about a hundred yards.

The days that followed were filled with gains and losses, but I kept on. On my son's first birthday I ran a super hilly 13.1

miles in two hours and eight seconds. My time won't win any awards, but it felt like a huge achievement to me. I started small when it didn't make sense and stuck with my small, silly habits. I built on them over and over until I reached my goal.

The beauty of that habit is that now I run *with* my son. He's eight, and he's the sweetest little running buddy. It's fun to think my running journey began when he was in my womb and now he runs beside me (sometimes holding my hand). It's such a joy.

That's an often-overlooked blessing of building great habits. They are passed on to those around us. My habit of running might very well be passed on for the next couple of generations. As a result, maybe my children and their children will live longer, healthier lives.

Habit building the right way takes time, but it is so worth it.

So what habits are you trying to build? If you want to wake up every morning and spend time with Jesus and you're starting at zero, download your favorite worship song on your iPhone, set your alarm for five minutes earlier than you usually wake up, and spend the first five minutes of your day worshipping and thanking God for who He is and what He has done.

After waking up and focusing on Jesus becomes a habit, add to it. Wake up ten minutes early, program your coffee maker, find a cozy corner to worship in, and read one chapter.

By starting with tiny habits, every habit you build onto the routine *reinforces* the previous one. And if at some point you hit a season in life that knocks you down, you'll have your first tiny habits to fall back on and then build back up.

The goal is that waking up a little early and focusing on Jesus first will be your default. It's what you can't wait to do when vacation, sickness, guests, or a crazy schedule throws you out of your routine. It's your comfort and your go-to.

Tool 4: Keystone Habits

I was *very* opinionated about making my bed as a child.

"Making my bed is dumb. Why spend all that time fixing it up, when I'm just going to get in it again tonight and *no one* is going to see it anyway?'

In what I can only attribute to childhood genius, I even went so far as to use my sleeping bag at night and then throw it in the closet in the morning. Voila! I never had to make my bed, and I never got in trouble for not making my bed.

Adulthood required me to give up the sleeping bag trick, but I still refused to make my bed.

I *thought* it was a waste of time.

I *thought* it was impractical.

I thought wrong.

One marriage and three kids later, my bedroom was a mess.

It seemed that unmade bed was a magnet for unfolded laundry, backpacks, Legos (that's always fun to discover at 3:00 a.m.), and everything else that didn't have a home. And certain children of mine have a habit of wandering into our room in the early morning hours carrying blankets, pillows, and stuffed animals. I didn't mind the morning snuggles, but I did mind the morning mess of bedding and toys.

It drove me nuts. But how could I ask my kids to clean up their beds if I didn't make my own?

So last year I decided drastic action was needed. I decided . . . to make my bed.

After a few weeks of this waste-of-time and highly impractical habit, I realized something. Making my bed made a huge difference in my day and my home. Because my bed was nicely made, I stopped dumping things on it as I walked through my bedroom. So did everyone else in my family.

I bought pretty baskets for my kids to put their blankets and animals in. The morning mess was gone. I kept my night table tidy to match my tidy bed. I kept the couch tidier because my bed and night table were tidier. One thing led to another, and the next thing I knew, my room was consistently clean. It felt peaceful. I could get in my bed at night, and if everything else had gone wrong that day, at least I knew I'd made my bed.

I know what you're thinking . . .

Wow. Bed making. This sure is captivating stuff, Kat. I'm on the edge of my seat here . . .

Stick with me. Author Charles Duhigg calls a habit like this a *keystone habit*—one small change that initiates a domino effect influencing everything around it.[8]

We change our lives the same way we build a bonfire. Start small until it catches, and add to the flame bit by bit. If you want to change your life, focus all your efforts on one keystone habit, and let it lay the foundation for growth in every other area of your life.

Tool 5: Keep It Fun

Frankly, if your new habit is not fun in some way, you're going to wear down your willpower eventually. How can you make what you do fun? Listen to an audiobook or podcast while you work out. Study a section of Scripture or a biblical topic that excites you. Listen to worship music that ignites your love for God, and memorize applicable verses. Use a fun planner or planning tools. Get a new calendar app.

The more fun we can add to our habits, the more quickly they'll become real, solid habits.

I had a hard time building a morning *God*-time anchor with my kids. We'd find things that worked for a season and then didn't work. What finally stuck was when I got each of my kids a mini composition notebook and a pack of colorful pens. Now each morning they sit down to read and journal with the pens in their new notebooks. The small size of the notebooks made it less overwhelming to write, and the pens made it fun.

Tool 6: Reward

Sometimes a habit is a reward in itself. The satisfaction of doing it or the natural results of completing it make it easy to do again. But some habits need a little kick. For me, that kick is grabbing a cup of coffee at the gym after my workout.

While I already have the reward of completing a workout and the reward of feeling my muscles getting stronger, there is something celebratory about getting that cup of coffee. It's like a little high five to myself for a job done. Notice I didn't say *well* done. I don't always have an awesome workout. Sometimes I just walk into the gym, ride the recumbent bike for a few minutes while checking my e-mail, and then leave. But I stuck to the habit, so I get my reward coffee. High five, Kat.

Tool 7: Habit Scripts

A habit script is simply a step-by-step plan for your habit . . . until it actually becomes a habit.

The three-minute morning is a habit script. We've broken

down the elements of *God* time, *Plan* time, and *Move* time into their most essential parts and provided a step-by-step plan. Of course, you can customize it however you like, but the core concept of having a "recipe" is the key.

If we want to build a morning routine and we just wing it each morning, we are more likely to fizzle out. By creating a habit script, we remove the frustrating and exhausting element of decision-making from our early-morning routine.

Meet Ray and the Minivan Effect

How does this all work? Why are tiny habits, keystone habits, choice architecture, and all the other tools important to the success of our habits?

It's all about the minivan effect.

Several years ago, Jimmy and I decided we were going to take the plunge into minivan ownership. We had two children with another on the way, and our love of long road trips led us to conclude that the survival of our children and our sanity required us to invest in a minivan.

As we researched and evaluated our options, it seemed that minivans were suddenly *everywhere*. When we were looking at buying a Toyota Sienna, we saw Siennas at the grocery store, at school, at church—everywhere. Then when we thought about the Honda Odyssey, suddenly, they seemed to be everywhere.

We'd never, ever noticed minivans before.

This is what I like to call the minivan effect, and it will explain why tiny habits, keystone habits, and habit architecture are so important.

Part of our brain, called the reticular activating system, acts like a nightclub bouncer for all the input coming at us at any given time. Right now, you're thinking about this book and what I'm saying. But you could also be thinking about how your clothes feel on your body. Maybe your shirt is itchy or your socks are too tight. You could be thinking about your breathing or the way the air conditioner is blowing. You could be thinking about that sound you hear in the background or the way your skin feels tight.

We are bombarded with input from all our five senses. Our brain, wonderful as it is, can't process all that input at once. Just as Taylor Swift, who seems to love meeting fans, can't possibly handle all the people coming at her in airports or on the street, your brain can't handle all the input coming at it at any given time. Just as Taylor Swift has bodyguards who manage who gets access to her, your brain has your reticular activating system to help you focus on just a few things at a time.

The problem is, our reticular activating system bodyguard—let's call him Ray—isn't the smartest guy on the block. Anyone can smooth talk his way into the inner circle. So if we see a cookie and start thinking about the cookies Grandma used to make, suddenly Ray is on high alert for cookies. We see cookies everywhere. The stop sign looks like a cookie. We smell cookies as we drive past a bakery. We remember that the convenience store has cookies. And we hyperfocus until . . . we get a cookie.

So the key to getting Ray to work for us and not against us is to put blinders on him. The less information we give Ray, and the more focused that information, the better things will get through so we focus on them.

This is where choice architecture comes in.

When we consciously set fruit on the table instead of a candy bowl, we are using choice architecture to help Ray focus on what we want him to focus on. We see the fruit and think about how hungry we are and how we really do like a good apple and, "Oh, look! There's one right there." Voila! A good choice made possible by choice architecture and our reticular activating system. On the contrary, if we surround ourselves with things we really don't want to focus on (candy, negative people, things like that), Ray will focus on those things, allow them through, and set us up for dangerous choices.

How can you use choice architecture to build your habits?

Keystone habits also help Ray because you're creating a big sign for him that says, "This is important. Focus on things like this." If Ray could talk, he'd be saying, "Help *me*, help *you*." Just as you set up your work environment to help you work, it's important to set up your habit-building environment to help you build good habits. And we do that by focusing on one important thing at a time.

As Kelly McGonigal, PhD, a Stanford University lecturer and author of *The Willpower Instinct*, put it, "If there is a secret for greater self-control, the science points to one thing: the power of paying attention."[9]

Now that you understand some habit-building tools, how will you use choice architecture, tiny habits, keystone habits, and your new buddy Ray to help you build your morning routine? (In the appendix you'll find a Habit-Building Quick Guide with practical examples of how to apply these tools.)

The Impact of Habit Building

That is why I am so passionate about Hello Mornings and the habit of starting your day with God. It is the greatest keystone habit.

It's like buttoning the top button on a shirt. If you button the top button right, everything else lines up. If you button it wrong, everything else gets out of whack. It doesn't take much to be intentional with that top button, but it does take a little more thought and attention.

Same with our mornings. It doesn't need to be complicated or time-consuming—just intentional.

There have been seasons when my morning habit was praying, "God, I want to want to get up and start my day with You. Help me."

That was it. The end. *Nada más.*

Pretty pathetic, right? I'm not writing this book because it was easy for me or because I float two inches off the ground with all my holiness. I stink. I'm a Bible study class dropout. I've started and not finished far too many in-depth Bible studies. I'm a poster child for low standards. But you have to start where you are with what you have.

I've found that I love writing down scriptures. So my base habit is to write a few verses from whatever book of the Bible I'm writing out at the time. Sometimes it's just two verses, but other times I write longer, get drawn into a passage, and study deeper. Sometimes I write my verses and complete a lesson from a Bible study I've gotten from a bookstore.

Perfection isn't my goal; progress and permanence are. I want to build a permanent habit foundation that grows every year.

The beauty of habits is that they raise our foundation. Every tiny habit we build shortens the distance to the ground when we fall off the wagon and makes it so much easier to climb back on and move forward.

nine

The Power of Preparation

"I was screaming and terrified on the inside. I didn't even know I was calm until everybody kept saying that. And so what I did is I went back to listen to the 911 tape to see exactly what I was saying and how calm I was. And to be honest with you, I didn't even recognize my own voice. And so I knew at that moment that it was God that guided me through that day."

A chapter about preparation might seem kind of boring, but Antoinette Tuff would tell you otherwise. On an ordinary Tuesday in 2013, at Ronald E. McNair Discovery Learning Academy in Decatur, Georgia, she was thankful that her life of faith, and even the pain of her personal story, had prepared her for the moment when she would step beyond her job as a bookkeeper, into that of a hero. She would save the lives of hundreds of school children as well as countless teachers and emergency responders.

"All of us have a purpose in our life. And so God prepares us all for one. That day was very important for me that every word that proceeded out of my mouth at that point in time could be life or death, not only for me and Michael Hill [the gunman] but for everyone in that building. And so I knew that that was the moment that I had to make sure that everything that I heard God say to me, was what I came out of my mouth with."

When an NPR interviewer asked her if being put in that situation made her question her faith, she replied, "No, 'cause I was too terrified to question him. I needed him [God] to talk every minute he [the gunman] was there. I was calling on him more than I'm calling on him any day. I was like, 'God, what we going to do now, what we going to do next, what do I say, how do I say it?' 'Cause remember now, he [the gunman] had already shot a bullet right there in front of my face, in the office, and it ricocheted. I'm sitting there literally [watching] him unfold mentally. You know, spraying bullets everywhere, loading up the magazines, you know loading bullets in his pockets everywhere. I'm actually seeing him self-destruct right there. So I knew that the power of my words had to be powerful."

Her words were so powerful, in fact, that she single-handedly talked gunman Michael Hill into laying down his weapons and ammunition and surrendering to officers. What she said was extraordinary. "It's going to be all right, sweetie. I want you to know I love you, okay? I'm proud of you. That's a good thing that you're giving up and don't worry about it. We all go through something in life . . . You're going to be okay. It's going to be all right."[1]

She spoke the words Michael needed to hear. She spoke the words few people could fathom saying to a man carrying an AK-47 and five hundred rounds of ammunition. She not only spoke them; she meant them. Her compassion and calm were noticed not just by Michael but by the police officers and even the president of the United States, who called her later to thank her for her courage.

Only God.

—————

What does Antoinette's story have to do with morning routines? It was a routine Tuesday morning for her. In fact, her life was relatively routine. Antoinette's professional experience had not prepared her for such extraordinary circumstances. She wasn't a Navy SEAL. She wasn't an Army Ranger or a trained policewoman. She was a bookkeeper whose husband of thirty-three years had just left her. She was a single mom who, only nine months before, had contemplated suicide after her marriage fell apart. She had no idea that her life, her words, her very wounds, would protect and save the precious children trapped in the school that day.

But God knew. And she knew God. And when asked what she hopes people learn from her story, she responded, "Make sure that you prepare yourself for a purpose. And when God calls your number, make sure that your heart is open to receive what directions he give you."[2]

Shift Your Preparation Perspective

Prepare yourself for a purpose. It's what we've been talking about, isn't it? We can't know exactly what our purpose is or how it will play out, but we can prepare. We can open our hearts to receive God's direction, and we can even prepare to make listening a daily habit. So when God calls our number, we'll be as ready as Antoinette Tuff.

When morning comes, the more prepared you are, the easier it will be to follow through on your morning routine. If you take a few simple steps, you can say *adios* to your snooze button and hello, morning! (See what I did there?)

If I'm honest, I love being prepared. I love packing the car before our big vacations, getting everything in order and placed most effectively for space and accessibility. I love preparing for each week and the clarity it brings to see it all in one place on my calendar. I love when someone needs something (a Band-Aid, hairspray, medicine), and, like Mary Poppins, I have it in my purse.

There is a wonderful satisfaction in being prepared. Can you remember a time when you were fully prepared for a school project or homework assignment or trip to the grocery store? You had all your t's crossed and i's dotted, and you felt unstoppable. Preparation makes everything else easier.

Set Your Preparation-Time Anchor

So how can we prepare for an effective morning routine? What can we do ahead of time to be ready?

The simplest thing you can do is to have a morning kit—a small collection of things you need for your routine. For the three-minute morning, that would consist of your Bible, water, and calendar. Some people keep their morning kit in a small bag or basket so they can take it with them. Others keep it at their morning "spot" in their house.

Kelly Gerber says, "I have my study materials and pens ready in the same spot (command central for my mornings). I charge the phone so it's ready to be my Bible and calendar and keep me going throughout the day."

Araceli C. Day says, "I have a specific corner of the house where I do my morning time, and my basket with all the supplies stays there (other than my planner). My wake-up alarm is programmed on my iPad, so as I head to bed, I plug the iPad on its stand on my dresser (away from the bed so that I have to actually *get out of bed* to turn it off!)."

Julie Atkinson Reynolds confirms, "I set a bedtime alarm, and make sure that my study materials and calendar are ready and waiting in my spot."

A morning "spot" is popular for three-minute morning users, but if you prefer variety and sometimes have your time on the porch or by the fireplace or in your bed, having a bag or basket makes it simple to be spontaneous.

Start Growing Your Preparation Time

Once you've prepared a morning kit, the next step is to consider how you want to grow your preparation; how you want to smooth the path to a great morning even more. This is the fun part. This is where we pamper our future selves. I like to think of it like having a guest, except the guest is my tired, grumpy morning self. I prepare candles, coffee, a cozy corner, and all the little accoutrements of an inspiring morning time.

Few things make waking up early more fun than having a little nook all set up, ready, and waiting for me to snuggle down and let God fill me up so I can live the day for Him.

If we put in the preparation beforehand, when the alarm goes off, the rest will be easy. Here are some key preparations we can make to give us the best possible opportunity to create a long-lasting morning habit.

The Night Before

The simplest way to prepare is to simply think about preparing. It doesn't get any easier than that, right? Mental preparations are the seemingly small things you need to do to ensure you actually get up and have your morning time.

You can set an alarm in the evening to just start thinking about going to bed on time or figuring out solutions for obstacles you face (for instance, if it's cold, think of putting a robe by the bed). You can also decide when you'll set your alarm; gather your Bible and study tools, exercise clothes, calendar, coffee, or tea; and set up your morning spot.

I find it incredibly helpful to spend a few minutes as I fall asleep thanking God for the day and then intentionally remembering why I am planning to get up with purpose tomorrow. Simply remembering that God has a purpose for you can be the spark you need to get you out of bed. Or remembering why you want to start the day with a few jumping jacks, not just because it's on your list and you feel as though you should but because you're blessed to be able to move—and the more energy you have, the better you'll be able to live your life well.

Honestly, I think your bedtime routine is almost as crucial

to the success of your mornings as your morning routine is. Here are some examples to get you started:

- Go to bed on time.
- Pack lunches.
- Prep breakfast (precook breakfast burritos or waffles and have them ready to heat up).
- If you have kids, have them set out their clothes and all school supplies.
- Lay out your clothes for the next day.
- Review your schedule for the morning.

What tasks can you do the night before that will simplify anything you might need to do in the morning?

_____

_____

_____

_____

Prep Your Family

If you have small children and your husband has agreed to "run defense" if the kids wake up during your morning time, thank him for that and ask if there is anything you can prep to make it easier for him if they do wake up. You might also offer to take over after your morning time so he can have his own morning routine.

If your children are old enough, remind them of their wake-up time and make sure they have morning resources to keep them busy if they wake up when you do.

If there is no one available to "run defense" for you, keep a mental list of activities your little one can do while you have your morning time, such as eating breakfast, playing with toys, or coloring.

We used to have a piece of paper with each kid's wake-up time next to a digital clock in their room. If the first number on the paper and the first number on the clock didn't match, then it was time to try to sleep or read quietly. When the numbers matched, they could come out.

Some special clocks have lights that change from red (stay in bed) to green (time to get up) for children old enough to understand the concept but too young to read. Some of these clocks also play music or a short story to keep children entertained when it's too early to get up.

Prep Your Tools

I'm a bit of a morning-spot supply addict. I love resources. Here are some of my favorites:

- Bible

    I use a New International Version Bible because I've had it for years, and all the pen marks and highlights make me happy. I've also started to use the English Standard Version.

    Whatever translation you use, I highly recommend keeping a highlighter or pen handy. There really is something special about a well-used Bible that inspires me to dig in.
- Notebook

    I've tried to use fancy notebooks, but for some reason, the thought of messing them up with my not-so-pretty handwriting stresses me out, so I use a super cheap spiral notebook from the grocery store for my Bible study.

Think through what kind of notebook might most invite you to write in it. A pretty journal? A legal pad? An old-fashioned diary? A plain notebook? Try new options until you figure out what keeps you going.

- Bible Study

    If you're using a specific Bible study book, keep that with your Bible and journal. Make sure to choose a study that will fit the amount of time you have available each morning. If you're not sure how to choose a study, start by asking friends or your pastor for recommendations.

- Clothes

    I like to make sure that my clothes are all ready for me in the morning. Frankly, I usually sleep in my work-out clothes, but I make sure a cozy robe and slippers are ready for me when I emerge from the warm cocoon of my bed.

    If you go to the gym or run outside, make sure your shoes, keys, phone, and jacket are all ready for you so you're not racing around the house in the dark looking for them.

- Pens

    I'm not gonna lie; I love a good writing implement. Gel pens, felt pens, ballpoint pens. I may be a little addicted. My absolute favorite pens are Pigma Micron, but I also like the Papermate InkJoy. Whatever pen you prefer, make sure you also have a good highlighter handy.

- Workout Equipment

    If you'll be using weights, bands, or a mat, make sure

everything you need is in the space where you'll be working out.

Prep Your Morning Spot

It's one of my favorite moments of any non-school day. As I sit in my closet office, affectionately known as my cloffice, reading and sipping coffee, I hear a quiet little knock, and the door slowly creaks open. Messy light-brown morning hair peeks around the corner, and my son's blue eyes light up when he realizes he woke up before his sisters and gets me all to himself.

He'll give me a sweet hug and then sit down on the little couchlike cushions behind me as I wrap him up in a soft blanket. I love making my children snuggly warm.

One by one, my kids wake up and come into my little five-by-five-foot space. They squish together with their books and breakfast, and at some point, I'll declare, "Twenty-six hundred square feet!" They all have their own rooms as well as the family rooms, but they find their way into my tiny little space.

It's not a perfect spot, but it's definitely cozy. On one side is my desk that faces and extends the length of the wall. My guitar hangs on my left, and directly in front of me above my desk is a magnetic board covered with a million sticky notes with quotes and messages from my kids.

Behind my office chair, opposite my desk, the wall is divided into two sections. On top hangs a long shelf the length of the wall, about four feet up. On it sits a cube of baskets where I keep most of my clothes, and a hanging rod is above that. Beneath that long shelf is a tiny sitting area covered in pillows, floor cushions, and blankets where my kids like to get comfy. And in the corner sit a few small weights ready for a quick workout.

A coffee machine with a collection of tea and hot chocolate complete the little space—a welcome treat on cold mornings.

My closet didn't always look like this. When I first started having my morning time in a closet, it was just that: a tiny closet where I sat on the floor under my clothes to read and pray. My introvert self needed a space where I could focus and read without fear of interruption or waking anyone up.

But as my habit has grown, I've made more preparations for my morning time. I have a place to sit (an actual chair!), something to drink, and everything I need to study, plan, and exercise.

The preparation I've done to create this space has made it inviting not only to me but also to my children. It has become a treasured space in our home.

Your morning space may look different. It certainly doesn't need to be in your closet. Maybe you have an actual *room*! Or maybe you prefer your living room couch or a cozy chair or the comfort of your own bed. (That option can be dangerous, though.)

Here are some ways to make your morning spot just right for you:

- Mug

  My grandmother had a mug collection. I remember seeing them lined up in the rec room in the basement, and I always wondered what the stories were behind each one.

  My grandmother isn't here to tell me about them, but I've started to build my own collection. There is something so sweet about sipping coffee from a mug with a story. Whether it was a gift from a friend or one we've picked up on our travels, I love having mugs that remind me of the life I've lived and those I'm living for. I keep a couple to choose from in my office for my morning coffee.

- Lighting

  Nothing is much worse than to be shocked awake in the morning by a harsh light. While it's a good idea to eventually turn on brighter lights to trigger a chain of signals in your brain to help you wake up, consider having a small, inviting lamp or book light at your morning spot to help you adjust.

- Candles

  Fact: I have an overactive fear of burning my house down. It's so obnoxious that nearly every Sunday I run back in the house as we leave for church because I need to make sure I turned my curling/straightening iron off. And now that I have teenage girls, I run through all three bathrooms making sure everyone turned everything off. Actually, I take pictures of the unplugged irons. Weird, I know. But I have this overactive fear . . .

  All that to say, while I love the concept of candles, I don't actually use them much. But I recently discovered battery-operated candles, and . . . I'm in love.

  The beauty of these little treasures is that they often come with timers. So I can set them for just a little bit before my normal wake-up time. Then the next morning, a little glowing candle cheers me on in my morning routine and welcomes me to my cozy little morning spot.

How amazing is that? Who doesn't want a little candle cheerleader?

- Music

  This one is huge for me. Music wakes me up, helps me tune my heart to Jesus, and stirs my soul. I have a morning worship playlist with some of my favorite current worship songs, and I have another playlist of old hymns that I enjoy.

- Warm drink

  Y'all, I've used everything under the sun for my morning time. I've had tea, smoothies, coffee, and water. I've used a coffee pot, a Keurig, a French press, a carafe of hot water, and a heater to get the water hot.

  I've made instant coffee, tea bag coffee, and last night's coffee.

  There are so many ways to prep a nice, warm drink without having to do a lot in the morning (or wake up anyone). Here is the simplest and cheapest: the carafe. Just get a small Thermos or carafe, and fill it up with hot water (or coffee) the night before. Then when you wake up, you can just pour your water (or coffee) and prep your drink. Simple. The other bonus of a carafe is that you don't have to worry about the coffee maker waking up anyone. Another option, if noise isn't an issue, is to use a programmable coffee maker and set it to be ready when you get up.

  Again, I like to have a small basket filled with different kinds of tea, flavored coffees, and hot chocolate. There is something oddly fun about ceremoniously selecting my morning drink. "I choose you."

- Snack

    I also like to keep a small snack in my morning spot because caffeine before breakfast sometimes makes me feel not so awesome. If caffeine on an empty stomach is an issue for you, too, here are a few quiet breakfast snack options:

    * Fruit: a banana is my go-to, but apples, oranges, and other easy-to-eat fruits work well too.
    * Breakfast bars: I love granola or fruit and nut bars. They taste amazing and are relatively healthy.
    * Crackers: I try to keep a stash of something I'm not as likely to eat so I know it will always be there even if I haven't refreshed my options lately. A small bag of crackers tucked in a corner ensures that I won't have to leave my morning time should hunger strike.

Whatever your morning space looks like, a few small preparations can simplify and enhance your daily routine and make it one of the most special parts of your day for you and your family. How can you make *your* morning spot inviting?

_____

_____

_____

_____

My Secret Morning Tricks

If you're afraid of waking your family when you get up in the morning, here is a simple trick I use to keep my family sleeping soundly. If you have an air-conditioning unit that has a schedule or a Wi-Fi app, set the fan to run a minute or two before your wake-up time.

Of course, you can also use a sound machine, but I've found the air-conditioning fan is a simple solution that many people already have access to in their homes. It does a wonderful job of adding plenty of white noise so any sounds you make are masked sufficiently.

If getting out of bed is difficult for you, one way to guarantee your emergence from the coziness of your cocoon is to use two alarms. I have one alarm on my watch that I set to go off first. It's a vibrating alarm (I sleep with my watch on). I like it because it only wakes me up. But because some mornings I need more than a gentle buzz to rouse me from sleep, I set a couple of backup alarms on my watch, all five minutes apart. Then I set a couple of alarms on my phone, each with increasingly annoying alarm sounds. Fortunately for my husband, my vibrating watch alarm usually wakes me up, and I turn the others off once I'm out of bed.

Having those backups helps me to be consistent, knowing that there is no way I'm going to sleep through all the alarms, and I might as well just get up when the first one goes off.

Now if you have children and want a foolproof alarm, set your second alarm and put it by your kids' bedroom door. I promise you'll fly out of bed when your first alarm goes off. No one wants their kids to lose a minute of precious sleep—partially for their health and partially to secure our solitary morning time.

Prepare for Obstacles

As you think through some of your biggest morning obstacles, whether that's a cold room or an alarm that's too easily snoozable, it's good to also prepare ways to overcome those obstacles.

Myquillyn Smith, blogger and author of *The Nesting Place*, shared:

> I found that one of the main reasons I hate to get out of bed is because it's *so warm in bed*! And I hate being cold. So I pave the way with warmth with a sheepskin rug next to my bed, fleece-lined slippers ready to slip my feet into, and a fluffy throw in my favorite spot in the family room. Knowing I can stay warm and cozy after I wake up is a huge motivator for me.

Honestly? There have been plenty of mornings when I've gotten up early to have my morning time, and I opened my phone and got lost in a social media spiral. When I was going to spend twenty-five minutes in worship and prayer, I spent it on Facebook and Instagram in coveting and discouragement. Not awesome.

One thing I do to combat the black hole obstacle of my phone is to set a timer as soon as I wake up. I leave my phone on the timer to remind me whenever I'm tempted to pick it up that I'm supposed to be spending time with Jesus and that the other things I was going to do "real quick" can wait.

I also use technology to overcome technology. A variety of Wi-Fi-connected devices can help parents manage their kids' Internet use. We have one of these devices, but I also use it to help *me* manage my own Internet use. I set a bedtime and a wake time for my Internet usage.

Technology can also be a blessing. I have worship playlists

on my phone, apps that help me study the Bible, and social media prompts that remind me to pray for my family.

Mountains can become molehills with a little preparation.

The Impact of Preparation

Andrew Wyeth, a twentieth-century American painter, once showed his brother Nat some drawings he was working on in preparation for his painting of Lafayette's quarters near Chadds Ford, Pennsylvania. There was a sycamore tree behind the building, and the drawings Andrew showed Nat were of the gnarled roots and trunk of the tree. Puzzled, Nat asked him, "Where's all that in the picture?"

"It's not in the picture, Nat," Andrew said. "For me to get what I want in the part of the tree that's showing, I've got to know thoroughly how it is anchored in the back of the house."[3]

Andrew could paint with confidence, accuracy, and authority because he had thoroughly prepared for every detail of his work, even the details no one would see.

We have no idea what today may hold. Today may blend into the next forty years as an ordinary day, or it may threaten everything you are—as one day did for Antoinette Tuff. The challenge here is to make the choice to prepare for our purpose—to stack the cards in our favor so when our alarm goes off in the morning, meeting with God and following His direction, whatever it may be, is the easiest and most natural thing to do. All it takes is a little preparation.

ten

Community and Accountability

In the late 1920s and 1930s, a series of experiments were held at Western Electric's Hawthorne factory in the suburbs of Chicago to determine whether changes in the work environment would improve worker productivity.

Elton Mayo formulated the experiments that began with simply increasing the lighting. Researchers noted that worker productivity significantly improved with the enhanced lighting. They went on to implement other changes, such as increased breaks and varied working hours. Every time they made a change, productivity improved.

While that seems logical, what is fascinating is that when all those measures were returned to their original states, productivity was at a fever pitch. In other words, employees were *most* effective after all the improvements were eliminated.

It doesn't make sense at first glance, but Mayo and his team discovered that it wasn't the changes that improved productivity, but rather the simple knowledge that their productivity was being measured. This became known as the Hawthorne effect.[1]

Think of those speed radar signs many local police departments place on busy streets so drivers can see their speed. Everyone knows these little signs cannot issue tickets, but when they are in place, compliance with posted speeds improves up to 40 percent.[2]

The right community and accountability can have a powerful effect on how we live our lives and how well our habits stick.

Shift Your Community Perspective

We talked a lot about understanding our season and situation in chapter 3. But another aspect of understanding our situation is recognizing the influence of our community. How will our current relationships positively or negatively influence our desire to build a morning routine and grow in our relationship with God?

We are better together. Home-court advantage is a real thing. When we have others on our side, cheering us on and holding us to a standard of excellence, we become the best version of ourselves.

Romans 12:4–5 says, "Just as each of us has one body with many members, and these members do not all have the same function, so in Christ we, though many, form one body, and each member belongs to all the others." We were made to need one another and to thrive within the context of community.

How can we shape our community in a healthy way? How can we surround ourselves with those who inspire and encourage us?

While much of our community is a result of where our jobs are or where we are born, we can still be intentional—we can reach out and connect, inspiring one another to seek God on a deeper level.

Whom do you look to for advice and inspiration? What part does social media play in your day-to-day life? If you need to build a stronger support community, invest intention-ally in your most life-giving relationships. Be bold and invite those who inspire you to coffee or dinner. Ask questions. Read books that inspire you. Read blogs or listen to podcasts that encourage you to grow. Encourage and invest in others, and be the sort of friend who cheers on others.

Can you think of a time in your life when the people around you caused you to live better than you would have on your own? Can you think of people in your life right now who influence you in that way?

Even if you feel as though you are alone, with the wonderful advent of the Internet, you can find community, even if it's on the other side of the world. Here's what Jen, one of our Hello Mornings friends, had to say:

> I joined Hello Mornings several years ago when I lived abroad as a Peace Corps volunteer. In my remote village on the edge of the Kalahari Desert, I lacked a good faith community. Hello Mornings quickly became an important part of my life, filling me socially and spiritually in a time when I feared church and avoided Christian community, for the most part. Once I returned to the USA, I contin-ued to participate in Hello Mornings, eventually becoming a Bible study group leader. Hello Mornings reminded me that a community of Christians is vital to any believer, and it gave me the courage to seek out real-life community. Now

I'm fully immersed in my local church, and it's amazing to see how much I have grown and changed, all starting with Hello Mornings. Having accountability through Hello Mornings has cemented my morning *God* time, which is now a nonnegotiable, enjoyable start to my day.

I love that story. Not only did Jen pursue community and accountability, she even pressed in when it felt uncomfortable. And through her small step of courage, God did an amazing work.

Set Your Accountability Anchor

Accountability starts with us. We need to begin by keeping ourselves accountable to what we say we will do. The thing about group accountability is that it depends on the group. It depends on their steadfastness, their commitment, their situations, and their relationships.

I believe that before we can invest well in others and receive the full benefit of community accountability, we need to do a little bit of work to take a step in the direction of our own commitment to growth.

How do we create self-accountability? By first knowing what we're accountable for. Answer these questions for yourself, and consider posting them somewhere to inspire and motivate you daily:

- What is my goal?

_____

_____

- Why am I doing this?

_____

_____

- What is my plan of action?

_____

_____

- What reward do I want to see?

_____

_____

- How will I reward myself when I get it done?

_____

_____

- How can I set up passive external accountability (charts on the fridge, daily posting updates on social media, and the like)?

_____

_____

Many women who decide to take our thirty-day challenge—I'll call them "Julie"—take an approach similar to the following scenario: To get started on her three-minute morning thirty-day challenge, Julie printed out our habit tracker and posted it on her refrigerator. She didn't have to say anything to her family, but she marked off each day as she completed it, knowing that her loved ones watched her progress and held her accountable to sticking with it.

Julie didn't have to ask anyone to do work. She just posted her progress where others would see it. You could post something similar on your refrigerator or on Facebook or on a blog. You could post it in the break room at work or to a group text chat.

Blogger James Clear writes a yearly report on his goals.[3] The simple act of knowing you might report the results of your goals is a huge motivator to pushing through on the hard days. The beauty is that we can do this and not feel as though we are asking too much of anyone.

Start Growing Your Accountability

The simplest way to get started with some accountability is to simply message one friend and say, "I'm doing a three-minute morning challenge and would love to have you join me. Simple, but powerful. Interested?"

Once you find that friend to join you—or a spouse, child, parent, or coworker—set your start date and commit to texting (or whatever form of connection you want) for thirty days. You don't need to be perfect and do the three-minute morning every day, but at least commit to texting.

If you don't have anyone you can do the challenge with, simply print out your tracker and post it where others will see it. Check off each day as you do it. It doesn't require anything of anyone, but you'll be motivated to stick with it.

Be committed to this simple step. Keep posting your habit tracker. Eventually, someone will be curious and may even join you. If you lose an accountability partner, be committed to finding another.

Gather a Group

Having a morning accountability buddy is great, but you can find even more accountability and inspiration in a small group of women dedicated to growth in the Lord and dedicated to one another. You might already have a community at your church or in your friend group or family. But many others don't have that. If that is you, don't be afraid to build your own group.

The beauty of the age we live in is that community can be found in so many shapes and forms.

- Local group

  It's rainy and cold here in Waco today. I'm snuggling with my hazelnut coffee in a small booth at Panera. Yes, snuggling with coffee. Don't judge.

  Ironically, as I try to write this chapter on community, community is the very thing keeping me from writing. The thing about living in a small Southern city is that everyone knows everyone. Well, practically. It's hard to go somewhere without running into a friend. I thought 6:00 a.m. would insulate me from too much conversation. And it sort of did. I haven't seen anyone I know, but apparently, 6:00 a.m. on a Saturday morning is prime time for friendly older farmers to congregate at Panera. I do love how they are so encouraging to one another. Sharing their hog-maintenance wisdom, offering tractor tips, and swapping stories.

  You know who's loud? Friendly, elderly farmers. You know who I didn't expect to sabotage my writing time at Panera? Friendly, elderly farmers. They are at two tables on either side of me . . . talking to one another. Too bad my book isn't about fencing, tractors, and how to keep hogs off your land.

Wait. It just got worse. You know who's louder than elderly farmers? Friendly elderly farmers on cell phones. I have a feeling that these folks would do just about anything for one another. I imagine they've spent many years meeting together on Saturday mornings. The sense of community is truly tangible. And loud.

There is so much value in investing in relationships and community.

- Long-distance group

The Hello Mornings group I'm a part of is made up of one friend I see almost daily, another friend I see a few times a month, and another friend I'm lucky to see every few years because she lives overseas. But we are in one another's lives praying for each other, encouraging one another, and spurring one another on.

There are so many ways to maintain real-life relationships long distance. With FaceTime, Skype, Voxer, WhatsApp, good old-fashioned phone calls, and myriad other apps and options, all it takes is a little intention to keep the lines of connection open.

- Online group

Sometimes we are in seasons or situations that don't allow for local or long-distance relationships. Sometimes we need to find those who might understand our unique situation in the online space.

This one can be sketchy. While building community online can be powerful—some of my dearest friends live all over the country and have met together only a few times—you obviously have to use a lot of discernment when building online friendships and sharing personal information.

I have experienced such encouragement and blessing from online friendships. I've also heard powerful stories of how our Hello Mornings groups have offered just the support and encouragement others have needed in a time of isolation in their day-to-day world.

Ways to Stay Connected

However you choose to gather your group, you can stay connected in many different ways. Most groups I've been a part of have used each of the following ideas to some extent:

- Meet in person

  If you have the time and space, a weekly meeting can be a wonderful way to build community. Some churches that do Hello Mornings meet regularly, and they've said it's the most powerful ministry happening in their churches. I've also been a part of a long-distance Hello Mornings group, and while our main connection point is online, it was very bonding to plan a one-time gathering.
- Apps

  Many apps allow you to leave text or voice messages for one person or a group. You can listen while someone is leaving a message, or you can wait and listen later. This is perfect for friends with different schedules or in different time zones. You can still talk and hear one another's voices, but you don't have to schedule to all be on at the same time.

- Skype, FaceTime, phone calls

    Real-time connection is always a wonderful option, but it's not always practical in our busy society. Combining a monthly Skype chat with daily online connection can be a great way to build group unity. There's something special about face-to-face communication (albeit on screens).

- Facebook, Instagram, social media

    Some Hello Mornings groups use a special hashtag on Instagram or Twitter. Others have a dedicated Facebook group where they discuss Scripture and encourage one another. Now with Facebook offering live videos within groups, and Instagram embracing live video and stories as well, we have more ways to use these tools to connect and encourage one another.

- E-mail and texting

    E-mail and texting are simple, straightforward ways to connect with your group. But if your group is large or very interactive, you might consider using a group texting app or using your e-mail providers' filter options to help manage all the messages coming in. (Gmail, for example, allows you to filter e-mails to certain folders to keep your inbox clean.) Since these are frequently used forms of communication, it's easy for group members to feel overwhelmed if they don't have a method for managing the messages.

But What If I'm Not the Leader Type?

Yes, there are many ways to be a participant. But what about a leader? You may be thinking, *Don't I have to be a leader-type to start an accountability group?* You may share the common misconception that, to lead a group, you have to be an assertive expert. While that might be true if you're teaching a class, leading and teaching are very different.

All a leader needs to do is be faithful and encouraging. If you wanted to lead a group of friends through the three-minute morning challenge or through a Bible study, you don't need to be an expert. You just need to faithfully show up and encourage others to do the same.

Teachers are like tour guides. They need to have all the information, answer questions, and be the experts. But a leader simply needs to take steps forward and ask others to walk the journey with her.

Whether you want to gather some friends to do a workout routine together, study the Bible together, or organize your planners together, you can be that positive influence just by inviting people.

Christi Wilson shared her story of leading a group:

> Before leading a group, I would maybe start a study, but I wasn't consistent. I never did each day. When I became a group leader, God impressed on me that I was responsible for each lady in my group. I'd better get in the Word and be prepared for questions, comments, and remarks that could come from the lesson. It made me accountable, which made me dig in God's Word and have a closer relationship with Him.

Christi grew up in church but never had a deep relationship with the Lord. Church was simply what she did. But when she started leading other women, God took her deeper than ever before.

Christi said, "I became co-leader last study. It has been one of the best things I have done."

There is power in walking in our weakness and letting God lead. No doubt, leading is stretching, but without stretching we don't grow.

Michi Bird is no stranger to stretching herself. This mom of three went back to college a few years ago and is on track to earn her second bachelor's degree the same year her oldest son graduates with his degree. She said:

> As a leader for one of the HM groups, I find myself being stretched not just by God, but by these beautiful sisters He has placed in my life. God may speak one thing to me as I read over the verses for the day and contemplate them, but He speaks something different to everyone in my group. When these ladies post how God spoke to them, it opens my eyes to how one verse can be interpreted and applied in so many different ways. God uses these women to help mold me into what He knows I can be and they stretch me more than I could ever do on my own.

What Should Your Group Look Like?

If God is calling you to lead a group, consider who you should invite to join you. Consider these qualifiers, and invite the following kinds of people.

- Anyone you believe can benefit. We want everyone in the group to grow.

- People who will encourage others. We want everyone to be cheered on.
- Those who tend to be faithful. We want the group to thrive, not dwindle.
- People who will engage. We want the group to connect.
- Those with whom you'd like to build community. We want to invest in relationships.

When considering how many people to include in your group, think about the personalities you're inviting and how conversational they tend to be (online and in person), and make your decision accordingly. An in-person group of six seems to be an ideal size to keep the group lively, but also allows plenty of time for everyone to share. I find online groups do best with no more than twelve (unless it's a particularly quiet group of people). Also consider your preferences. If you don't want to spend a lot of time on your device in an online group, limit your size so you're not constantly having to keep up with what everyone shares. It's best to start small and add as necessary.

If you want to start a Hello Mornings group, it's simple. Just type the following sentences into a text message, social media message, or e-mail, and send it to the people you've chosen.

Hey! I'm doing a 3-Minute Morning Challenge to help me get in the habit of Bible study, planning, and healthy choices. It's super simple but powerful. I'd love for you to join me. Interested?

Easy peasy.

Please remember that not everyone will be able to accept.

It's not a reflection on you personally, but rather their season in life. Instead of feeling discouraged, be inspired by their self-awareness and courage to live within healthy boundaries.

What to Do in an Accountability Group

As the leader, the way you structure your group needs to be life-giving and manageable for you. It can be as simple as texting each other in the morning to check in, or you could meet weekly for deep discussion. You could connect online and ask a daily question, or you could talk on the phone regularly to stay accountable. What resonates with you? Here are some options:

- Deep questions

     Determine several thought-provoking questions whose answers move people forward in their journey of growth. Here are a few to consider:
     * What are your goals for this week?
     * How did you do with your goals last week?
     * How can I pray for you?
     * What obstacles can we help you brainstorm solutions for?
     * Were you honest in all your answers? (We used to ask this in my college church accountability group, and, sadly, it's really helpful.)
- Daily check-ins

     Sometimes all you need for a group is a daily check-in. No need to go deep or ask big questions—just saying "hello" and "how are you?" each morning reminds everyone of their morning routine and makes them want to stay on track. Just showing up is a highly underrated ministry.

How to Keep Others Accountable in a Healthy Way

Group accountability can be a bit of a dance. Just as it's important to know ourselves before building a new routine, it's important to be willing to learn about each person we are inviting into this journey. Some people need a lot of detailed accountability, while others simply need reminders and inspiration. Take the time to figure out where each group member lands on that spectrum.

When I was in college, I was part of an accountability group that was pretty hardcore. If we didn't do what we said we were going to do, we had to clean someone else's college apartment bathroom. Granted, we were a group of girls, so it wasn't as bad as some college apartment bathrooms, but it was still some serious accountability.

I also had a friend who came to know the Lord when she was in her early twenties. She grew up in a small country in eastern Europe. She was so excited about her faith and her growing walk with God that she and her friends committed to giving one another their entire salary for that week if they didn't do what they said they would do.

Now that is serious.

Please hear me: you don't need to do that. I don't even recommend it. But I want you to understand the heart behind it. She grew up never hearing about Jesus, and when she came to know Him, her life changed. She was deeply determined to live fully for Him, no matter what it took.

Most of you won't need that level of accountability. Some of you might need to hire a life coach or a counselor to stay accountable and to do so in a healthy way.

The goal here isn't to be super intense or sacrifice the most.

The goal is to grow in our relationship with Jesus and in our understanding of His Word. Each of us will do that in different ways, and it's important that we understand what will help us thrive.

Gretchen Rubin, author of *Better Than Before*, identified four types of people as it relates to personal growth:

Upholder—accepts rules, whether from outside or inside. An upholder meets deadlines, follows doctor's orders, keeps a New Year's resolution. [I am an upholder, 100 percent.]
Questioner—questions rules and accepts them only if they make sense. They may choose to follow rules, or not, according to their judgment.
Rebel—flouts rules, from outside or inside. They resist control. Give a rebel a rule, and the rebel will want to do the very opposite thing.
Obliger—accepts outside rules, but doesn't like to adopt self-imposed rules.[4]

Rubin went on to say that each type has its own pros and cons, and it's important to see the types on a continuum rather than as a black-and-white label. Most of us have a tendency to respond to rules in one of these four ways, but we don't always do so.

As we discussed in chapter 3, it's important to know what works for you. If you are a rebel, then a strict accountability group might send you running the other direction, but a daily connection point with friends would keep you inspired. If you are an obliger, then a strict accountability group might be just the thing to help you get where you want to go.

We are all different. We have different motivations, inspirations, and life situations. Find what works, and work it.

The Guilt-Grace Vortex and How to Avoid It

The greatest saboteur of group accountability is guilt—more specifically the downward spiral of guilt and grace. I like to call it the guilt-grace vortex.

It usually goes something like this: I have a legitimately hard week and don't do the things I said I would do. I come to the accountability group meeting feeling guilty and confessing my shortcoming. Then someone else tells their story about how they didn't do what they had planned either. It's hard to keep other people accountable to things we haven't done ourselves, so it's our tendency to then just give one another "grace." The problem is that we often fall short of our plans, especially as we trial-and-error our way through building a morning routine.

All too often, the group slowly stops keeping one another accountable. I've done this more times than I can count. If we truly want what is best for someone else, we can't just let them down when they've asked us to hold them up. So I was thrilled when life coach Carey Bailey taught me a better way than the guilt-grace vortex.

Ask questions. Instead of just holding people to a rigid goal that they are struggling to meet, spend time talking through the obstacles and challenges they are facing. Brainstorm ways around those obstacles, or help them ratchet down their expectations and slow down their progress to a speed that allows them to thrive rather than just survive. Rather than simply saying, "Oh well we didn't get it all done this week. Bummer," we ask questions and help one another get to the core reasons *why* we didn't get it done. When we know the reasons, we can work together to build a solution for their morning that will work.[5]

Simply asking *why* to each answer can quickly get to the root issue, but try other questions as well:

- What made you decide that?
- Why was that hard to do?
- How can we avoid that in the future?
- How can we make the on-ramp for that goal/habit easier?

In this way we can truly be "as iron [that] sharpens iron" (Prov. 27:17).

Small Changes, Big Results

The benefits of surrounding ourselves with others on the same journey is undeniable—even scientific.

In 2009, the UK tax authorities added one small sentence to their collection letters. The sentence simply said that most other people were paying their taxes. That's it. And that one simple addition "led to the collection of £560 million of the £630 million debt targeted for recovery by Her Majesty's Revenue & Customs." That was a 30 percent improvement over the previous year![6]

It is human tendency to do what those around us do. That's why it's so important to be intentional about your community—your circle of influence. Love the people God brings into your life, pursue friendships that push you to Jesus, and gather friends who raise up one another.

To whom will you be accountable; how will you connect?

_____

_____

_____

_____

The Impact of Accountability

She was in seventh grade, and I was in fifth grade. She was twelve, and I was ten. If you remember back to grade school, two years are an unfathomable social gap to cross. But time after time, Becca bridged the gap. And for reasons only God can explain she chose to invest in my life for the next, well, thirty years. And counting.

In junior high, she included me in conversations and let me tag along. In high school when she was prom queen and I was all kinds of freshman awkward, she invited me into her circle of friends. When she was in college, she let me come visit and taught me to play the guitar. I was in her wedding. She was in mine. She listened and discipled and saw me as more than I ever thought I could be. She showed me what it was to faithfully meet with Jesus, pray, persevere, and love others.

You would not be reading this book without the influence of Becca Nelson in my life.

She usually rolls her eyes a little when I talk like this. "Oh, you weren't a dork." "I wasn't that cool." "You were fun to hang out with." ' We were good friends." "I didn't do anything special."

Here's the thing: we rise and fall to the expectations of those around us. I think God must have given Becca some special rose-colored Kat glasses to mask my social ineptness and then placed her in my life to walk me through some of my hardest seasons. I think He knew the power of a friend who calls us to higher things.

I became a better person because I was around a better person.

Build your morning routine within a community of people who will encourage and inspire. Whether you have to build that community yourself or step into one that's waiting, it's worth the effort. It's worth the commitment. It's worth the vulnerability. It's worth it, because He is worth it.

eleven

Call to Action

What if you could wake up every day feeling like a six-year-old on Christmas morning? Do you remember what that felt like? The hope? The anticipation? The unbounded belief that *anything* was possible?

When we were six, we fully believed there could be a real pony under the tree. Or a new bike. Or maybe even a puppy. When we were six, Christmas morning couldn't come soon enough. No matter how groggy we felt when we woke up, within seconds it hit us: "It's Christmas!" Our hearts flooded with excitement and our footie-pajama-clad feet flew to the living room.

I'm not six anymore, but I have three children, and I love seeing their eagerness and joy on Christmas morning. All year long they write in their wish lists—plain spiral notebooks transformed into hope chests. They scribble in them, paste in pictures, and highlight favorite toys. They constantly refine them, itemize by price (oh, yes, they do), and build their anticipation for the big day. As they fall asleep on December 24, their dreams are filled with all the wishes they hope to find under the tree Christmas morning.

But on December 25, 2014, something was different. I didn't wake up to the usual flow of children whisper-yelling in my ear, *"Mama! Wake up! It's Christmas! Get up!"* (times 3,982). There was no one sitting on top of me, breathing their morning breath in my face, eye-begging me to get out of bed.

Instead, I leisurely walked down the hall to find my children sitting on the *opposite* side of the living room from the Christmas tree and the piles of wish-list dreams come true.

My ten-year-old daughter, Allison, lay on the couch reading a book. Jackson, my seven-year-old, played chess with his cousin; and my twelve-year-old daughter, Anna, sat cozily on the couch . . . crocheting.

Books, chess, and crochet.

I looked at them. And then I looked over at the gifts under the tree. I looked back at my oblivious children. Back to the gifts. Back at them.

"Um . . . Merry *Christmas?*"

Maybe they forgot?

With an absentmindedness uncommon on this particular morning of the year, they replied, "Merry Christmas, Mom."

Incredulous, I teased, "What are you doing? Do you realize what day this is? It's *Christmas!*"

I wasn't ready for them to be so grown up, so patient. I said, "This isn't what kids are supposed to do on Christmas morning. This is what grown-ups do. This is how your dad and I act. All cool and nonchalant."

What happened? They were supposed to be begging us to open presents. They were supposed to be bursting with excitement.

"Where's your childhood wonder? The joy? The excitement? You're like . . . you're like . . . old-people kids! Remember your wish lists? Those notebooks you've been writing in all year? Remember *all the things* you've been dropping not-so-subtle hints about for the past eleven months? Those toys you've been wishing for? It's all *right* there. Right *over there* under the tree, just waiting for you."

And yet my forty-year-old children were playing chess, reading books, and crocheting a scarf. Don't get me wrong, I love my old-people kids, and I'm thankful Christmas means much more to them than the presents. But that memory has served as a wonderful example to me.

Everything they wanted, hoped for, dreamed of all year long was within reach. It was all *right there* under the tree. Their greatest wishes were already purchased, they were already theirs, just waiting to be unwrapped.

My Wish List

I may not write them down in an itemized spiral notebook, but I have a mental list of wishes:

- I wish I weren't so insecure.
- I wish I didn't feel so overwhelmed.
- I wish I were more self-disciplined.
- I wish I were a more gracious wife.
- I wish I were a more patient mom.
- I wish I were a more thoughtful friend.
- I wish I had more faith.

- I wish I were more fervent in prayer.
- I wish I walked with God more closely.
- I wish . . .

I have all these wishes, and yet I wake up in the morning and start my day checking Facebook or reading e-mail. I hit the snooze button one too many times and oversleep. I forget that everything I need, the Holder of all those wishes, the One who meets my every insecurity and fear, He's *right here.*

Every morning. Right here. Waiting for me.

Six-year-olds don't hit the snooze button on Christmas morning. Who wants to snooze when so much goodness awaits? Treats to eat, presents to open, and cousins to play with? It's easy to wake up on days filled with hope and expectation.

What if we felt like that every morning? As if anything were possible? What if we could wake up like six-year-olds on Christmas morning—every morning?

We can.

The Possibility

I have felt overwhelmed, beaten down, and like I'm all-around failing at life. But when I was at my lowest, I began to realize how much possibility my life holds. It doesn't matter that I'm already fortysomething years old.

A moment of embarrassing honesty? I haven't quite laid down my Olympic dreams. To this day, every two years when the Olympics roll around, I start researching Olympic age restrictions and US and Filipino dual citizenship laws, and I try to determine whether I could qualify in some obscure summer or winter sport in either the US or the Philippines.

It doesn't matter (or occur) to me that I've never played the sport. Or that there are no winter sports in Central Texas. It doesn't matter that my chances are one in a million.

It's *possible*, and that possibility thrills me. That possibility, however absurd, has kept me in shape the past forty years on the off chance the Olympic snowboarding team will call and say they need a scrawny Asian woman to round out their roster.

Do You Believe?

The Bible says that with God, all things are possible (Matt. 19:26). Do you believe that anything is possible in your life? Do you believe God can—and wants to—do important things in and through you?

I know. Sometimes life feels humdrum, and days slowly roll by. But the fact is that each one of us has something meaningful to accomplish in life that no one else can. God created us uniquely to fulfill a specific story in this world.

Your life matters. No matter how small, insignificant, unorganized, or visionless you feel, there never has been anyone like you, and there never ever will be. God is not a redundant creator. And whether you recognize it or not, there are people you're meant to love. You have lives to influence, words to speak, work to do, truth to share, and peace to offer.

Maybe the person you encourage today will be the person who speaks the very same hope into someone else's darkness twenty years from now. Maybe the child in whom you inspire a love of science today will discover the cure for cancer. Maybe the person you hold the door open for at the store today will be reminded of the power of small kindnesses.

The truth is, we haven't a hint of the width and breadth of our influence.

And as long as we are alive, we have a purpose to fulfill. And every day is bursting with hope and possibility. Life is not meant to be lived passively. We are meant to show up for life. We are meant to show up prepared. And the only way to truly prepare is to connect with the One who made us so we can be ready with the words we're meant to speak and the actions we're meant to take.

Fighting Distraction

It's easier said than done, though. We live in a distracted, divided world. We are bombarded with information and responsibilities and decisions around every corner. As each day progresses, it gets fuller, and the things that are truly important are drowned out by the seemingly urgent messages being thrown at us.

We stop thinking about what is possible and think only about what is pressing.

I don't know about you, but I'm tired of feeling like a used and abused ping-pong ball at the end of the day. How can we stop feeling sideswiped and reactionary? How can we live with purpose and intention?

How can we make time for the most important things?

I've asked myself all these questions. Maybe you have too. Whether you feel you're at rock bottom, or you simply want to embrace all that life has, the solution is the same. We need to start well.

How We Start Matters

Think about it. How we start matters. How we start a relationship, how we start a job, how we start our day . . . it matters.

Have you ever tried to recover from a bad morning or a bad first impression? How we start makes everything afterward easier—or harder.

When I was at my lowest point, bombarded by all the things I thought I should do, I chose to focus on one simple thing. Start each day well. In the midst of my overwhelming desperation, I realized that the right start can change anything.

It has taken time. I certainly haven't built my morning routine perfectly. I've learned a lot along the way, but through much trial and error, I uncovered methods that built the foundation of a lifelong habit.

And an amazing thing happened. I began to wake up excited about the day ahead. I rediscovered the possibilities. I was able to get the most important things done first. My heart and head felt ready for the day.

Some of the biggest moments of my life can be directly traced back to this simple habit of a morning routine. I have truly come alive. And you can too.

Now That You Know, What Will You Do?

We've covered a lot of information in these pages. We've shifted our perspectives on what *God* time is, why we plan, and why our health is important. We've learned to set a simple three-minute anchor for a *God, Plan, Move* morning routine. And I've given you a variety of incredibly practical tools for building a grace-filled, life-giving morning routine.

So my question to you is, now that you know, what will you do?

Will you choose to bring your fish and loaves before God each day (see Mark 6)? Will you choose to be okay with the little you might have and pursue the deep impact of faithfulness?

Your journey ahead won't be perfect. You'll have hard days and harder days. You'll have mornings when it all clicks and other mornings when it feels as though the world is conspiring to keep you from meeting with Jesus. Some days you'll be aching to dive into the Word, and other mornings you'll just sit and stare.

Whatever you encounter, keep pressing on. Be persistent. Pray for a passion for the Word. Pray for a powerful prayer life. Ask God for wisdom in planning and the ability to make wise choices about your health. Petition Him to become a woman who not only hears the Word but also lives it by giving Him glory, loving others, and serving the least of these (see Matt. 25:40).

There are so many stories in Scripture about persistence:

- In Luke 11:9, Jesus told us to ask, seek, and knock, and the door will be opened to us.

- In Luke 18, Jesus told us about the persistent widow who pleaded with the judge day and night until he relented. And then He encouraged us to be steadfast in our prayer.
- Galatians 6:9 says, "Let us not become weary in doing good, for at the proper time we will reap a harvest if we do not give up."
- Second Thessalonians 3:13 reads, "And as for you, brothers and sisters, never tire of doing what is good."
- James 1:12 says, "Blessed is the one who perseveres under trial because, having stood the test, that person will receive the crown of life that the Lord has promised to those who love him."

We are not only building the habit of meeting with God each day; we are also being persistent in our pursuit of Him.

Homecoming

My daughter Allison is twelve, going on thirty-nine. She plays tennis, loves to bake, and reads incessantly. The other day I walked out of my office and saw her on her school iPad. She quickly clicked away from what she was doing. What had she stumbled upon while using her less-restricted-than-we'd-like school device?

I sat down and asked to see what she'd been watching. With a sheepish look, she opened the YouTube app. The sidebar was filled with videos. She looked at me and said, "I watch them whenever I have free time." They were soldier-homecoming videos. Soldiers surprising their children. Soldiers surprising their spouses. Soldiers surprising their siblings. One after another she started showing me her favorites.

Y'all, I bawled for thirty minutes straight. They were all so precious, but the ones that got me the most were when soldiers surprised their parents. Fathers and mothers, grown men and women, weeping and embracing the children they knew might not have come home.

Mothers overflowing with gratefulness and joy to be in the company of their children. Fathers looking with love and pride into the eyes of their children. Presence is irreplaceable. Despite technology, nothing can match face-to-face connection. One-on-one time with our loved ones.

I believe God rejoices when we choose to come to Him. I believe He is unrelenting in His pursuit of you, and that each morning you meet with Him is a homecoming.

So here is my challenge. My throwdown. Do whatever it takes, starting today, to surrender each day to God with the three-minute morning. You can shape those three minutes however you like; just come before Him with a sincere heart, a desire to grow, and a commitment to persistence. In the midst of His grace, fight to be faithful and fight to grow.

I can't wait to see what great things He'll do with your willing heart.

What's Next?

Your Hello Mornings journey doesn't end here. In fact, this is only the beginning. I'd love to meet you and introduce you to the amazing Hello Mornings team and the thousands of women on this journey with us. We want to support you, encourage you, and grow with you.

I challenge you to share this book with someone, to invite her to do a thirty-day three-minute morning challenge with you and, perhaps, even scale up your morning routine together.

As you learn and take action, I pray that by God's grace, every area of your life will truly come alive. That you'll wake up each morning like a six-year-old on Christmas, seeing a day full of promise and possibility. Remembering that the Holder of all your hopes and dreams is waiting for you. Right here.

We don't have to wait for a new season or a new year to start fresh. As Anne of Green Gables said, it's "a new day with no mistakes in it yet."[1]

Today is a new start for you.

Are you ready? It's time to wake up *for* your life, not just *to* your life.

Appendix

Resources

This is an important moment. This is when you decide to either close the book and move on or embrace the momentum and ignite your morning routine. Revolution is simple. If you're ready, check out these next steps to get you going in the right direction:

1. Sign the My Morning Revolution commitment in the next section, and keep a copy of it in your journal or Bible.
2. Invite a friend or loved one to do a thirty-day three-minute morning challenge with you.
3. Gather a group and download our leader's guide (and other resources) at HelloMornings.org.
4. Join our community at HelloMornings.org. We want to cheer you on!

My Morning Revolution

Make your commitment official. Take these words to heart, and sign and date this statement so you can remember the day your mornings changed.

I understand that God doesn't want my perfection; He wants my pursuit. So I've decided to let go of my guilt about my mornings and pick up the grace offered on the cross.

I understand that time with Jesus is the core of everything I need. So I refuse to be mastered by time but instead choose to make room for the Master of time.

I understand that God is not a redundant Creator. He made me for specific purposes. So I choose to prayerfully plan my days to pave the way for His purposes.

I understand that I am created in the image of God. So I choose to focus my fitness on increasing my energy to bring glory to His image rather than mine.

I understand that building small habits creates solid growth. So when guilt rears its ugly head, saying I'm not doing enough, I'll cling to the Grace that crushed guilt beneath His heel.

I understand that meeting with Jesus daily will change my life forever. So I choose to start each day with God, no matter how much or how little time I have, simply because He is worthy.

Now to him who is able to do immeasurably more than all we ask or imagine, according to his power that is at work within us, to him be glory in the church and in Christ Jesus throughout all generations, for ever and ever! Amen.

—Ephesians 3:20–21

Signed:_____

Date:_____

Quick Review List

The Three-Minute Morning Essentials

God Time: Pray Psalm 143:8
Plan Time: Review calendar
Move Time: Drink a glass of water

The Three Steps of Change

1. Shift your perspective
2. Set your anchor
3. Start growing

Perspective Shifts

It's not about a checklist.
Focus on persistence, not perfection.
Planning is something we do with God.
Connect the dots.
Don't sweat the small stuff.
Fitness is about energy, not image.
Small habits are the foundation of transformation.
Preparation makes us ready for God's purposes, not just our plans.
Change comes more quickly in community.

How to Grow Any Area of Your Life

Step 1:   Track
Step 2:   Trade
Step 3:   Try

Seven Powerful Habit-Building Tools

1. Triggers
2. Choice architecture
3. Tiny habits
4. Keystone habits
5. Keep it fun
6. Reward
7. Habit scripts

The Hello Mornings Big Bible Study Idea List

The best thing about this list of ways to study Scripture is that it can be used with *any* section of Scripture. So, if you want to do a study on 1 Corinthians 13 or look up all the verses on faith, just use this list to build your own Bible study method.

Reading and Writing

Read. Simply read the passage. You can read it in your head or aloud, thoughtfully and slowly, or in another translation.

Write. As I mentioned earlier, writing out scriptures is a wonderful way to slow down and absorb each word. As we write, our brain creates thousands of new neural pathways, allowing us to more deeply consider and remember what we learn.

Identify key verses. In the passage you're reading, which verse holds the nugget of wisdom? Which verses explain the transformation of the main characters? Which verses speak most to you in the season you're in right now?

Highlight, underline, bracket, circle, jot. In this digital age, there is something therapeutic about words on a paper page and a pack of highlighters or colored pencils. I always loved looking at my grandmother's Bible filled with highlights, underlines, notes, and circles.

Take time to circle commands, underline truths, or highlight key verses in your favorite shade of pink. Bible study can be fun and colorful!

Observe. Let your inner Nancy Drew loose. Uncover the five W's of the passage: who, what, when, where, why, and (don't forget) how. It's amazing how much we can learn from just naming the different elements of a passage or story.

Illustrate. In the margins of your Bible, or in a journal, get creative! Design word art focusing on a key point. Sketch the setting, characters, or theme.

Outline. Feeling more cerebral than creative? Outline the story or teaching. Highlight the main points and the subpoints to develop a greater understanding of where the author was coming from and what he was trying to communicate.

Personal paraphrase. Sometimes we learn best by teaching. Imagine you had to share the heart of the passage with a group of friends or a class of children. How would you paraphrase it? Or try paraphrasing it by incorporating your story into it and the things God has done in your life. You could even paraphrase it by simply inserting your name everywhere the passage has a generic pronoun.

A word on Bible studies. One problem people face is finishing a Bible study and not having a core habit or a plan for what is next, and then simply falling out of the habit of studying the Bible. While it's important to plan ahead, perhaps even making it a fun tradition to decide each year what you'll study, it's also key to always keep your anchor habit. That way, when life gets crazy, you keep solidifying your habit.

Respond

A great way to dig deeper into Scripture, of course, is to ask a few simple questions. You can think about the answers as you read, or you can write down your responses in a journal.

The Bible truly comes alive when we consider and pray about how God wants us to apply it to our own lives.

Questions to consider:

- What does this say about God?
- What does this say about the church?
- What does this say about me?
- What truths are in this passage?
- Does this passage lead me to confess anything in prayer?
- What should I pray?
- What actions should I take?
- How can today be different because of this passage?
- What are some journaling questions I could take from this?
- What is the lesson from this passage?
- Which key verse should I memorize this week?

Research

Every page of Scripture offers so much to be learned. But sometimes we can take our study to a new level when we start flipping the pages and learning the story behind the story.

Here are a few things you can research about the passage you are studying:

Author. Who wrote this passage? What do we know about him and how he fits into the story of the Bible? What were his circumstances? Why did he write it? To whom was he writing? Where was he when he wrote it? What had God done in his life to compel him to write this passage?

Background. What was the background of the passage? What story or theme was introduced in previous verses or chapters of the book?

Audience. Who was the audience the author was writing to? Why was this written to them? How do you think they responded to it? How would you have responded?

Context. What was happening in history at the time the passage was written? What was the culture where it was written? How did the culture or the historical circumstances influence the author? Are there any grammatical rhythms or clues identifying or strengthening the author's meaning or ultimate intent?

Cross-reference. If you have a Bible with cross-references (or you are using an online resource), look up all the verses associated with the passage. What can you learn from them, and how do they influence the text?

Commentaries. Read the commentary in your Bible, in commentary books, or at a trusted online source, such as BlueLetterBible.org, Biblehub.com, or BibleStudyTools.com, to gain even more insight into the passage.

Translations. Read the passage in multiple Bible translations. How do they differ? How are they the same? What new truths can you glean from the variety of perspectives?

Maps. Maps may be available in your Bible or online related to the passage you're studying. Follow the journey of the main characters. Look up modern-day pictures of the locations Research how long their journeys may have taken or any obstacles they may have encountered in their travels, culturally or geographically.

Word study (original language). Brush up on your Greek and Hebrew and study the passage in the original language by using an interlinear Bible that includes the Greek and Hebrew words from which the English version was translated.

The Habit-Building Quick Guide

When we get down to the nitty-gritty of habit building, I'd like you to take these seven habit-building tools and stack them on top of one another to create a foolproof plan to stick to your new habit.

Of course, a tool may work better for some habits and not as well for others. The idea, though, is to use as many of these tools as makes sense to create backup layers for your routines.

Seven Powerful Habit-Building Tools

1. Trigger
2. Choice architecture
3. Tiny habit
4. Keystone habit
5. Keep it fun
6. Reward
7. Habit script

Habit-Building Examples

I don't use every tool for every habit I try to build; I just evaluate what I'm trying to accomplish and pick the right tools for the job. Here are a few examples:

Morning *God* Time

1. Trigger: my morning alarm on my phone. I labeled the alarm "War Room" (after the movie title) to remind me of why I'm getting out of bed and what I'm going to do.
2. Choice architecture: my cloffice (closet office). It has everything I need for my morning time: blankets, coffee, candles, my Bible, pens, a notebook. It makes it easy to get started.
3. Tiny habit: I only have to write one verse.
4. Keystone habit: Praying Psalm 143:8 as soon as I wake up.
5. Keep it fun: I enjoy working at trying to improve my handwriting while I write out scriptures. Can't say I'm making much progress, but I enjoy working on it. I also like to use colorful pens.
6. Reward: connecting with God. Peace for my day.
7. Habit script: I start every morning the same way. I write out scriptures in a spiral notebook. It wakes me up and helps me really think through what I'm reading. After writing, I will do some more in-depth Bible study. Right now I'm reading a book on prayer, and then I spend time praying.

Morning *Plan* Time

1. Trigger: this simple habit follows my *God* time.
2. Choice architecture: I keep my calendar and overall

to-do list on my phone so it's easy to keep up to date and to access. I keep my weekly planning on paper because it's easy to see at a glance. Copying it all down in one spot each week helps me remember what we have going on, and it keeps me off my phone during the week.

When I start work, I dive into deeper project-specific planning. On Saturday or Sunday, I usually have a bigger planning time for the week.

3. Tiny habit: just looking at my calendar.
4. Keystone habit: (I don't use one here.)
5. Keep it fun: I like writing out my to-do list and calendar items with pretty colored pens. It makes up for my terrible handwriting.
6. Reward: not forgetting things as much.
7. Habit script: sometimes consists of just looking at my calendar and jotting down a few things in my planner. But when possible, I like to flip through the front pages of my planner that include my personal mission statement, my long- and short-term goals, my current projects, and my daily to-do list.

Morning *Move* Time

1. Trigger: this simple habit follows my *Plan* time.
2. Choice architecture: I sleep in my workout clothes and prep a water bottle before bed. After I take my kids to school, I do my workout.
3. Tiny habit: drinking my water.
4. Keystone habit: (I don't use one here.)
5. Keep it fun: I'll often check my e-mail or social media while I'm stretching.

6. Reward: energy!
7. Habit script: It usually consists of drinking a bottle of lemon water or stretching. I also often review my sleep at this time. If I didn't sleep well or enough, I brainstorm how I can get better sleep. Adequate rest is the first line of defense in our health and our energy levels.

My Daily Workout

1. Trigger: my existing morning routine.
2. Choice architecture: choosing to drop my son off last to make going to the gym at his school crazy easy.
3. Tiny habit: I just need to walk in and do one exercise—one rep or one minute.
4. Keystone habit: I have a favorite exercise that I love to do because it immediately makes me feel stronger. Doing that one exercise always makes me want to keep going.
5. Keep it fun: I never work out for longer than twenty-five minutes. Normally it's fifteen to twenty minutes. Is that going to give me an overnight transformation? Nope. Have I missed a day this year or dreaded going even once? Nope. The best part is, with this doable and enjoyable routine, I can still see significant improvements in my strength and overall fitness.
6. Reward: coffee after my workout.
7. Habit script: bike first for five to ten minutes, then do a simple rotation of upper-body and lower-body exercises.

Daily Green Smoothie

1. Trigger: making breakfast for my kids.
2. Choice architecture: I buy frozen smoothie mixes. So easy.

3. Tiny habit: (I don't really use one here since this is an easy habit for me.)

4. Keystone habit: (I don't use one here.)

5. Keep it fun: I used to make my own smoothies and put tons of extra greens in and all kinds of extras. But, frankly, they tasted nasty. So I keep it fun by allowing myself to buy a smoothie mix that tastes amazing and add in a few things to boost the nutrition and energy it provides.

6. Reward: tons of energy. I feel good about how I start my day.

7. Habit script: make my smoothie and immediately wash all the blender parts so I'm ready for the next morning.

Acknowledgments

Book writing is a team sport. While my name might be on the cover, this book wouldn't exist without the wisdom, coaching, and encouragement of many. In no particular order, I'd like to thank . . .

My Family

Jimmy, you single-handedly made this book possible. Thank you for your encouragement, sacrifice, and wisdom. Anna, Allison, and Jackson, thank you for suffering through the extra screen time, fast food, and unenforced chores while I finished this book. I'm sure it was terrible. But, really, thank you for the hugs, music, and encouragement every step of the way.

Dad, Chris, and the entire Slager/Balaja family, as well as my wonderful Lee family, I'm so thankful for all of you!

Aunt Rufe and Esther Sandee, thank you for reaching out so I could meet my wonderful Monares family.

The Hello Mornings Team

Melissa, Joyce, Jessica, Ali, Kristee, Ayoka, our GEMs, Group Leaders, and Katie Orr, thank you for all you've invested in Hello Mornings.

Don Jacobson, agent extraordinaire, thank you for your wise counsel and patience with all my questions.

Debbie Wickwire, what a tireless encourager you are. Thank you for investing in me.

The entire W Publishing team, it is such an honor and privilege to work with you.

Anne, Chic, and Patricia, thank you for your faithful prayers and listening ears.

Kellye, Blair, Lexia, and Liz: the best book club ever. Books optional.

Chrystal, Sarah, Jamie, Kristen, and Logan, I would have lost my mind without y'all.

And special thanks to the Voxer Girls (retreat soon?), my Hello Mornings podcast cohost Heather MacFadyen, Sarah-Jane Menefee, Carey Bailey, Betsy Zenz, and Sally Clarkson.

Nctes

Chapter 1: Setting the Stage

1. As transcribed by the author from "A Great Sports Father and Son Relationship Jim & Derek Redmond," WorldSportsTeam, YouTube, June 16, 2013, https://www.youtube.com/watch?v =DOvsYF6GVU8.

Chapter 2: Do Our Mornings Matter?

1. *English Oxford Living Dictionaries*, s.v. "possible," https://en .oxforddictionaries.com/definition/us/possible.
2. Maika Leibbrandt, "Why Being One in a Million Really Isn't That Special," August 28, 2013, CliftonStrengths Coaching Blog, http://coaching.gallup.com/2013/08/why-being-one-in -million-really-isnt.html.
3. Author's own calculation made at https://www.hackmath.net /en/calculator/combinations-and-permutations?n=34&k=34&o rder=1&repeat=0.
4. Carl Haub, "How Many People Have Ever Lived on Earth?" October 2011, Population Reference Bureau, http://www.prb .org/Publications/Articles/2002/HowManyPeopleHaveEver LivedonEarth.aspx.
5. L. M. Montgomery, *Anne of Green Gables* (Toronto: Bantam, 1987), 245.

Chapter 3: Are You Ready?

1. For additional resources and downloads for tracking your time, check out author and time management expert Laura

Vanderkam online at http://lauravanderkam.com/books
/158-hours/manage-your-time.
2. The currently available online version of the Smalley/Trent
personality test is geared toward marriage relationships
(smalley.cc/images/Personality-Test.pdf), so we've chosen a
paraphrased version that is more broadly applicable.
3. Adam Alter, "Why It's Dangerous to Label People," *Psychology
Today*, May 17, 2010, https://www.psychologytoday.com/blog
/alternative-truths/201005/why-its-dangerous-label-people.
4. Claire E. Adams and Mark R. Leary, "Promoting Self-
Compassionate Attitudes Toward Eating Among Restrictive
and Guilty Eaters," *Journal of Social and Clinical Psychology*
26, no. 10 (2007): 1120–44, as cited in Kelly McGonigal, *The
Willpower Instinct* (New York: Avery, 2012).
5. Beth Moore, "Grace," Living Proof Ministries Blog,
September 17, 2013, https://blog.lproof.org/2013/09/grace.html.

Chapter 4: Laying the Foundation for Your Morning Routine

1. Roy F. Baumeister et al., "Ego Depletion: Is the Active Self a
Limited Resource?" *Journal of Personality and Social Psychology*
74, no. 5 (1998): 1252–65, https://pdfs.semanticscholar.org/33e2
/50711d6eab5a4cf3a5543a67c7179f376af3.pdf.
2. Anthony Trollope, *An Autobiography* (1883; repr. Newcastle
upon Tyne: Cambridge Scholars Publishing, 2008), 63.

Chapter 5: God Time

1. William H. Willimon, "Attendance," *Pulpit Digest*, https://bible
.org/illustration/attendance; also see Philip Hallie, *Lest Innocent
Blood Be Shed* (New York: Harper and Row, 1979), 85.

Chapter 6: Plan Time

1. I've created a workbook that will walk you through writing
your own mission statement. Check it out at http://www.hello
mornings.org/missionstatement.

2. Laura Vanderkam, "Are You as Busy as You Think?" *Wall Street Journal*, February 22, 2012, https://www.wsj.com /articles/SB10001424052970203358704577237603853394654.

3. Quoted in William Yardley, "Zig Ziglar, Motivational Speaker, Dies at 86," *New York Times*, November 28, 2012, http://www.nytimes.com/2012/11/29/business/zig-ziglar-86 -motivational-speaker-and-author.html.

Chapter 7: Move Time

1. A. M. Williamson and Anne-Marie Feyer, "Moderate Sleep Deprivation Produces Impairments in Cognitive and Motor Performance Equivalent to Legally Prescribed Levels of Alcohol Intoxication," *Occupational and Environmental Medicine*, 57 (2000): 649–55, http://oem.bmj.com/content /oemed/57/10/649.full.pdf.

2. "Why Is Sleep Important?" National Heart, Lung, and Blood Institute, February 22, 2012, https://www.nhlbi.nih.gov/health /health-topics/topics/sdd/why.

3. "Blue Light Has a Dark Side," Harvard Health Publications, September 2, 2015, http://www.health.harvard.edu/staying -healthy/blue-light-has-a-dark-side.

4. Sumathi Reddy, "The Best Temperature for a Good Night's Sleep," *Wall Street Journal*, February 22, 2016, https://www .wsj.com/articles/the-best-temperature-for-a-good-nights-sleep -1456166563.

5. Joshua J. Gooley et al., "Exposure to Room Light before Bedtime Suppresses Melatonin Onset and Shortens Melatonin Duration in Humans," *Journal of Clinical Endocrinology & Metabolism* 96, no. 3 (March 2011): E463–E472, https://www .ncbi.nlm.nih.gov/pmc/articles/PMC3047226/.

6. Arlet V. Nedeltcheva et al., "Insufficient Sleep Undermines Dietary Efforts to Reduce Adiposity," *Annals of Internal Medicine* 153, no. 7, (October 5, 2010): 435–41, https://www .ncbi.nlm.nih.gov/pmc/articles/PMC2951287/.

7. Erica L. Kenney et al., "Prevalence of Inadequate Hydration

Among US Children and Disparities by Gender and Race/Ethnicity: National Health and Nutrition Examination Survey, 2009–2012," *American Journal of Public Health* 105, no. 8, (August 1, 2015): e113–18, https://www.ncbi.nlm.nih.gov/pmc/articles/PMC4504329/.

8. Donald Sommerville, "Battle of Marathon," *Encyclopedia Britannica*, accessed March 21, 2017, https://www.britannica.com/event/Battle-of-Marathon.

Chapter 8: How to Build Habits

1. Charles Duhigg, *The Power of Habit* (London: William Heinemann, 2012).

2. Dan Pink, "The Power of Habits—and the Power to Change Them," DanPink.com, March 2012, http://www.danpink.com/2012/03/the-power-of-habits-and-the-power-to-change-them/.

3. James Knierim, "Basal Ganglia," Neuroscience Online, UTHealth, http://neuroscience.uth.tmc.edu/s3/chapter04.html.

4. Anne N. Thorndike et al., "Traffic-Light Labels and Choice Architecture: Promoting Healthy Food Choices," *American Journal of Preventive Medicine* 46, no. 2, (February 2014): 143–49, https://www.ncbi.nlm.nih.gov/pmc/articles/PMC3911887/.

5. Drake Baer, "The Secret to Changing Your Habits: Start Incredibly Small," *Fast Company*, May 12, 2013, https://www.fastcompany.com/3022830/the-secret-to-changing-your-habits-start-incredibly-small.

6. For more information, you can visit Dr. Fogg's website at http://tinyhabits.com/.

7. Theodore Roosevelt, *Theodore Roosevelt: An Autobiography* (New York: The Macmillan Company, 1913), 365.

8. Charles Duhigg, The Power of Habit (blog), http://charlesduhigg.com/the-power-of-habit/.

9. Kelly McGonigal, *The Willpower Instinct* (New York: Avery, 2012), 236.

Chapter 9: The Power of Preparation

1. Michel Martin, "How One Woman's Faith Stopped a School Shooting," interview with Antoinette Tuff, January 31, 2014, *Tell Me More* (radio show), National Public Radio, http://www .npr.org/templates/transcript/transcript.php?storyId=268417580.
2. Ibid.
3. Kenneth A. Brown, *Inventors at Work* (Redmond, WA: Microsoft Press, 1988), 375.

Chapter 10: Community and Accountability

1. "The Hawthorne Effect," *Economist*, November 3, 2008, http://www.economist.com/node/12510632.
2. David Veneziano et al., "Guidance for Radar Speed Sign Deployment," Tables 1, 2, and 3, Western Transportation Institute, http://www.westernstates.org/Projects/COATS /Documents/TRB2012/Radar%20Warrants_TRB%20Paper _20112-1-23_FINAL.pdf.
3. James Clear (blog), http://jamesclear.com/annual-review.
4. Gretchen Rubin, "Four Personality Types: Which One Are You?" GretchenRubin.com, January 7, 2013, http://gretchen rubin.com/happiness_project/2013/01/four-personality-types -which-one-are-you/.
5. Author's personal interview with life coach Carey Bailey, December 9, 2016, in Parker, Colorado.
6. Roger Trapp, "How the Little Things Can Make a Big Difference," *Forbes*, August 29, 2014, https://www.forbes.com /sites/rogertrapp/2014/08/29/how-the-little-things-can-make-a -big-difference/#1a98d776f8bd.

Chapter 11: Call to Action

1. L. M. Montgomery, *Anne of Green Gables* (New York: Puffin, 2008), 245.

About the Author

Kat Lee is passionate about teaching others how to jump-start each day with a grace-filled, life-giving morning routine. She is a writer, speaker, podcaster, and founder of HelloMornings .org. She and her husband, Jimmy, live in Waco, Texas, with their three children. Stay connected with her at TheKatLee .com.